To Kelly
This is your
time.

Benavidez

THE 7 SECRETS TO
A LIFE OF
MEANING

Insights on living with passion and purpose

Ian Percy

The Seven Secrets to a Life of Meaning
Insights on living with passion and purpose
by Ian Percy

Copyright © 2001 by Ian Percy

Published by: Inspired Productions Press LLC
Scottsdale, Arizona

First edition

Cover design by Henry Corona, Miami, Florida
Inside layout by Ad Graphics, Inc., Tulsa, Oklahoma

Printed in the United States of America

Library of Congress Card Number: 00-111964

ISBN: 0-9707140-0-9

PRAISE FOR
THE SEVEN SECRETS TO A
LIFE OF MEANING

"Ian did a masterful job of providing the framework for people to methodically discover who they are and how to move forward. *Seven Secrets* is the perfect book for those looking for their own spiritual answers and direction."

– Gary Yamamoto, PhD.

"Our workplaces are filled with people looking for meaning in their lives and work. *Seven Secrets* is the key for them to more clearly discover that meaning, thereby accessing energy, productivity and creativity many times beyond what is currently available to them."

– Tom Gegax, author of *Winning in the Game of Life*.
Co-Founder and Chairman, Tires Plus stores

"Ian creates deeper meaning for grateful audiences around the world. Likewise, this book is like an intimate walk in the garden with a wise and insightful counselor. I will return again and again to meditate on his words and apply his advice."

– Jim Clemmer, author of *Growing the Distance* and
Pathways to Performance

"This book is about stepping BOLDLY & FULLY into LIFE!"
– Martin Rutte, Co-Author, *Chicken Soup for the Soul at Work*

"The issues you address are not talked about nearly enough, especially your points about building your life around purpose and passion. And your thoughts on 'irritation' were particularly powerful because it described me exactly. I saw my life in your book so dramatically. I loved your honesty."

– **Paul Henderson**, Hockey Legend and
President, Leadership Ministries

"There is no more important quest in one's life than the search for Meaning. The Why's of life always overpower the How's. This book will shorten your search and may well dramatically change your life. If it does, it will be for the better...much better. When you find meaning in your life you add value to your life. And the rest of us will be better off because you did it."

– **Jim Cathcart**, author of *The Acorn Principle:*
Know Yourself – Grow Yourself

"You make the interrelations between business realities and spirituality striking. Passion in business is no different than passion in life. This book transcends both worlds well. A very good read!"

– **Kevin Francis**, President, JetForm Incorporated

"Ian's warm, personable style engaged me on every page. I found many fresh ideas and approaches that are helping me – and my coaching clients – make better life choices."

– **Steve Straus**, Certified Master Coach

"With *The Seven Secrets to a Life of Meaning*, Ian Percy continues to challenge his readers to move deeper within and beyond. His relentless search for meaning, for both individuals and corporations, is a joyous journey filled with insights, challenges, information – and wonderful stories! This book is going to help a lot of people shift their lives toward more depth and meaning."

– **Grady Jim Robinson**, author of
Did I Ever Tell You About the Time...

IN HONOR OF *TIME*

This book, along with my love, is dedicated to our children Karen, Nathan, Erin and Ryan. All young adults as I write this. All at the front end of discovering what a life of meaning will mean to them. When I think of the four of you I cannot help but wish that I had some of my time back again. But it doesn't work that way. This is *your* life-*time*. Do not throw away a minute of it. Take your *time* – take *all* of your time – and look for that which is precious and meaningful in every moment and in every day. Nothing will thrill me more than to see you stand tall and declare to Creation that God has sent you to change things. You have already changed me, and I love you for it.

With this book I also honor our parents. They have all taken *their* time and have filled it with discoveries, adventures and service like few have. My parents, Harry and Joy Percy, devoted their time to serving God in Africa and Canada with a commitment rarely seen. I pray that my father, now suffering from Alzheimer's disease, will somehow know that I have written this book and that I honor him with it. My pride in my mother's strength grows daily with each mountain she climbs. You both have helped shape the meaning of my life. I also have the best in-laws in the universe – Bud and Babe Gardner – who welcomed me like a son from the moment I met them. Without a doubt they will continue to make the most of *every* minute of their time, showing us all what it means to live life to the fullest.

I honor many of my "co-participators" – people like Linda Tarrant, Jane O'Callaghan, Renee Strom, Andrea Gold, Nancy Vogl, Martin and Farah Perelmuter, Jim Clemmer, Jim Hennig, Eileen McDargh, George Morrisey and so many others who continue to encourage me in the meaning of my work. Valued friends like Susan Suffes and Randy Gage who helped me so much with this book. I couldn't share my time with more wonderful people.

And I honor my wife Georgia with whom I will spend the rest of my time. Without you life would lose much of its meaning. I love you.

IDP

TABLE OF CONTENTS

What is the most difficult question in the universe?

You can't find your destiny alone! Here's how to be sure you have surrounded yourself with the people who can help you.

Chapter Two

There is more of a pattern to your "journey to meaning" than you might think. Once you know the way, the journey is so much easier!

Nothing worthwhile has ever happened without someone first getting irritated and restless – and then deciding to make the world a better place. What has angered you may hold the secret to your destiny!

Many of us tend to get stuck in our current situation. The problem is that the more you stay focused on what has already happened, the less able you are to create your richly imagined future. Free your self to your future!

Chapter Five
Your Richly Imagined Future

This is where you find the Seven Secrets! Seven wonders that serve as wise signposts, pointing you toward your destiny.

Chapter Six
Unleashing Your Power

You can't go on a cruise unless someone unties the boat! Learn to positively disrupt your life so you are free to go where your destiny calls. Your future requires you to take your life apart as well as put it together.

Chapter Seven
Making Courageous Choices

Life is about choices! Deep within us we know the choices we need to make. All we need is the courage to make them! Knowing the meaning and purpose of your life may be a choice away.

Chapter Eight
Learning From the Wisdom of Others

Meet seven wonderful and very different people who have found their purpose. Hear their stories and learn how they came to know why they are here on earth.

Other Highly Recommended Explorations

About the Author

Other Inspirational Products

INTRODUCTION

Nothing you will ever do is as important as discovering the meaning of your life!

N ot only is it the most important thing you will ever do, it's also the most difficult. So difficult in fact, that I originally planned to title this book *The Most Difficult Question in the Universe*. Actually, I had a lot of fun with that title. I'd tell people the title and they would stand in silent expectation for a moment. If I didn't say anything further, they'd ask, "Well, what is it?" Sometimes I'd jokingly say, "$27.00!" Most of the time, however, I'd ask them what they thought the most difficult question was.

That may be a good way for us to get acquainted as well. What do *you* think is the most difficult question in the universe? It could be one of those weird dizzying questions like, "Can water wet itself?" or it could be the old tree falling in the forest with no one to hear it debate. Or it could be a deeply philosophical slash scientific question like, "When does life begin?" I don't know if a definitive answer to that would help either the Pro-Choice or Pro-Life folks out or not. Maybe life doesn't begin or end; maybe life just *is*. Or how about philosophical slash theological questions: "What happens after we die?" and "Does it matter what religion you choose?" or "If God is love, how come innocent people suffer?"

One of the greatest minds of our age, Stephen Hawking, adds another difficult question in his book *A*

Brief History of Time: "Why does the universe go to all the bother of existing?" Thinker and theologian David Hilbert said the most difficult question is, "The infinite! No other question has ever moved so profoundly the spirit of man." (This is where I nod knowingly as if I actually understand what Hilbert's question is.) Apparently, no one has come forward with answers so clear that the whole world nods and says, "Yup, that's it!"

I wonder if Colin Percival knows what the most difficult question in the universe is. He's the Canadian teen who, according to *The Province* newspaper in British Columbia, calculated the value of pi to the five-trillionth digit. That sounds pretty difficult to me. Of course he did use twenty-five computers all linked by E-mail and running on programs he wrote himself. Apparently the five-trillionth digit is 0. I guess he did it because pi was there.

Mathematics rather grandly lends itself to this sort of discussion. Many extremely intelligent and insightful people insist that all creation is based on mathematical principles. One especially difficult area of fascination has had to do with "perfect numbers" which mathematicians have been studying since ancient times. In 300 BC Euclid wrote: "If as many numbers as we please beginning from a unit be set out continuously in double proportion, until the sum of all becomes a prime, and if the sum multiplied into the last make some number, the product will be perfect." This will stretch my mathematical capacity, but here is an example: $1 + 2 + 4 = 7$, which is a prime number. Euclid further says multiply seven by the last number in the sequence, which is four, and you get twenty-eight, which is a perfect number. The difficult question is: "What is the largest perfect number?" The largest one so far was discovered on January 27, 1998. It contains 1,819,050 digits! I'd write the number out for you but it would take over 600 pages to do so and I don't think you'd read it.

This, however, is child's play compared to the $7 million challenge offered by The Clay Mathematics Institute of Cambridge, MA, which will pay a million dollars for each solution to seven specific problems. These "stand out as great unresolved problems of the 20th century" says Princeton University professor Andrew Wiles. These problems have names, like The Poincare Conjecture, The Navier-Stokes Equations and The P versus NP Problem. One of them, called The Riemann Hypothesis, looks like this:

$$\zeta(s) := \sum_{n-1}^{\infty} \frac{1}{n^{s}},$$

Makes you want to get out the old pad and pencil, doesn't it? The people who know me realize that I barely understand a word of what I have written in these last couple of paragraphs. I'm still trying to figure out how long it would take two trains to pass each other if one left New York traveling west at 60 miles an hour and the other left Seattle traveling east at 70 miles an hour. I just wish I was as smart as the student who wrote on his math exam, "According to my calculations, the problem does not exist."

Mathematics gives us some very difficult questions. But unless numbers are your life, perfect numbers do not seem to have much to do with our day-to-day existence, at least not in our awareness. And the chance of winning the seven million is remote to say the least.

It seems to me that the most difficult question for us must have something to do with the pounding of our hearts, our limitless imaginings, what is as close to us as life itself. That means it can be nothing other than life itself. **So the most important and most difficult question in the Universe is:**

What is the meaning and purpose of my life?

No answer is more essential to your well being and happiness than knowing what you are meant to do with your life. But this book cannot *tell* you the answer any more than a fortune cookie can. If it were that easy, we'd *all* know the meaning and destiny of our lives. Sadly, most of us don't, and most of us never will. I am thrilled that you are not in that category.

Back when I was starting this book, I showed my working title, *The Most Difficult Question in the Universe,* to a potential literary agent. With what I thought hinted at disdain, he said, "People don't want questions, they want *answers*!" Fair enough, but isn't that the great trap of life? I didn't think of it in time to use it on the agent, but I later recalled the comment from the influential French literary critic Roland Barthes who said, "Literature is the question minus the answer." We often don't have the patience to understand the question. We just want someone to give us an answer, a quick fix. But how can an answer make any meaningful sense when you don't understand the question in the first place? That would be like me coming up to you and saying, "The answer is seven." It is very predictable that you are going to say, "The answer to what?"

There are endless ways to ask the same question. What is my destiny? Who am I? Why, in all this universe, is there a Life in my name, in my shape, with my experiences? What am I bringing to creation, or am I here just to take something away? In what way will I leave this world a better place? What am I supposed to do with my life? What is the "WHY?" of my life?

Three letters form the most complex and difficult question known to human kind. It is the first question we learn to ask as children and yet most people go through their entire life without answering it. Without an answer there simply is no foundation on which to live. Every "why?" is significant. They are the moment-by-moment experiences and re-directions that began with your incarnation. They include questions that range from, "Why was I born to these parents?" to "Why did I buy this book instead of the *Dilbert* one?" There is no end to them.

Larry Pike, Chairman of Union Central Life Insurance, a truly wise corporate leader and thinker, read a draft of this manuscript and suggested that perhaps the question ought to be, "Why not?" When Larry makes a thoughtful suggestion, I give it serious consideration. However, given the intention of this book, I am going to stick with "Why?" Here's why.

"Why not?" is a powerful question that can energize us to unlimited possibilities. Why not learn to scuba dive? Why not volunteer a year of service with a relief organization of some sort? Why not go to medical school at forty? Why not write your first novel at seventy? Why not dedicate your life to finding a solution to the homeless problem? Why not anything? Why not everything? "Why not?" is like walking on your life's path and coming across a thousand signposts, each sending you to a different place. "Why not?" puts your spirit in motion. Having recognized the value of "Why not?" the fact remains: *movement* isn't enough, we also need *intention.*

Our innate need for intention is what connects us to the most difficult question of "Why?" Knowing "Why?" gives us purpose so we can choose which of the signposts to follow. This book is about finding our life's purpose and meaning. "Why not?" offers us propulsion, "Why?" offers us purpose. It is not about what career you should choose or about analyzing your personality. **It is about finding** *meaning* **in your wonderful and amazing life.**

There are, I discovered, **Seven Secrets to a Life of Meaning**. You will find them quietly hidden in the middle of the book, in Chapter Five. Early readers of this manuscript found that a little peculiar. After all, I could have written one chapter for each secret and had it all presented simply and neatly. However, if I've learned anything, it's that discovering the meaning of your life is anything but simple and it is certainly not neat.

We have all seen the imagery of a seeker climbing a treacherous mountain in order to hear the wisdom of an old sage living at the peak. You, too, will have to climb your way through several very important and difficult issues before "the secrets" will make sense to you. Remember also, that once the seeker heard the wisdom he sought, he had to go back *down* the mountain or there would have been no value in gaining the wisdom. Likewise, you will have to work your way up to the secrets, and you will have to work your way "back" to use them in your everyday life. There are no easy paths to discovering the meaning of your life. What kind of "secrets" would they be if they were just laid out on a table at the Base Camp? People would take them because they were easy and free, but they wouldn't know what they had, and the value would be lost.

Nor will you find this to be a book filled with gentle and flowery thoughts. (However, there is a little of that, because we need a good story or poem every once in a while.) And while this is a deeply intimate book, it is also tough. You will go beyond theoretical concepts to concrete actions that will guide you toward actually *doing* something about discovering the reason for your *being*. Communication guru Ron Arden says, "Hope without 'how' is an empty promise" and not wanting to give you an empty promise, I suggest "Actions" at the end of each chapter designed to help you integrate the lessons of the book into your own life. You may or may not need that help. However, I do encourage you to at least read these "assignments" because I have included additional insights in them that lay a foundation for the succeeding chapter. Whether or not you choose to actually *do* any of the suggestions is, as always, totally up to you.

I have tried to write this book straight out of my heart and life. I write because that is the best way for me to find the answers I seek. At times during the process of writing I felt the filtering and second guessing that comes when one tries to ensure that every step of the thought-flow is clearly and logically spelled out and defensible. The effort reminded me of the tag attached to my new briefcase. "The blemishes in the leather," it read, "are a natural part of the cowhide and contribute to the unique charm of the product." Should you find such blemishes as you read, think and reflect along with me, I ask you to regard those occurrences as part of the "charm" of our exploration.

Most of my energy and attention was spent trying to connect with you, the reader. I wondered if you have experienced the same "stuff" that I have been through and what you might be going through right now. I wondered what you would say and ask if we were actually sitting together. So the flow of this book is based on all of those imaginings. If I have been at all successful, I believe we will have a meaningful connection. I am truly looking forward to it.

Ian Percy

Chapter One

BRINGING YOUR PASSIONS TO LIFE

What do you really want?

The materially-oriented among us will tick off their fantasies: a Ferrari, a beach house, a 72-inch digital television system. Others look at those who win millions of lottery dollars and wonder why that can't be them.

If we are physically limited in some way, we want to be well, to be done with radiation, to see, to hear, to walk again, to go through just a single day without pain. Athletes want to win. Propeller heads want a minimum 50 terabytes hard drive, 1 gigahertz processor, 40x DVD ROM, a DSL modem and 1024 mb RAM. Environmentalists want a world in which humans cease to destroy creation through greed and thoughtlessness. In some inner cities kids want to walk to school safely.

It struck me that, generally, we spend so much of our lives accumulating things – education, clothes, friends, money, notoriety, position – that we don't make time to discover what it is we *want* for our lives. That's like eating before you see the menu. We accumulate and do things without a purposeful reference for them. How can we know what is relevant and what is not?

For example, do you remember *any* time during your schooling where someone encouraged you to quietly reflect on the intimate meaning of your life and then, when you had done so, asked, "Now, how can we as a school system help you fulfill that meaning?" When was the last time an employer pulled you aside and compassionately asked you if the company had created a context in which you could find a significant outlet for your creativity and passion? What about your parents? Did they simply encourage you to just find a decent *job*, or did you have discussions about what would bring *meaning* and *significance* to your life? If you are a parent, are you like me? Do you find yourself impatient with the ambiguous or non-existent direction in your older children's lives? Don't you wish they'd just decide what they want and get on with it? When you were their age, you had finished your formal education, were married, had both kids and were an accountant. The other day I heard that the average age of a "kid" finally leaving home is almost thirty years old. That's 30 – three-zero!

If we have finally found a comfortable path on which we at least *seem* to be gathering the desires of our hearts, it is very easy to be critical of those who are still wandering. In our smugness we can sometimes act as though it was our own wisdom and clever planning that placed us in such a fortunate place. Instead, let's make a commitment to be absolutely straight with each other throughout this book. If we are blessed right now it is probably through the sheer grace and generosity of God who chose, for a reason we may or may not know, to smile down on us. Should you not wish to give God any credit, you must chalk your good fortune up to unbelievable timing, amazing luck or just being in the right place at just the right time. When most of us think back over how we got "here," we will recall maybe a half-dozen crucial turns in the road. A mere flip of a coin would have meant a totally different life experience.

Consider:

- If your dad hadn't been transferred, you wouldn't have been put into that new grade three class. But if you *hadn't* been, goodness knows when another teacher would have helped diagnose your dyslexia.

- Your older brother was forced to take violin lessons and hated every minute of it. Hoping you'd ruin the instrument, he said you could play with it as much as you wanted. It has become your career and your passion. Could it be that your parents had somehow received a mystical message that one of their children was meant to play the violin but just were confused about which one?

- You didn't make the track team so you tried out for football and are about to start your third year as a pro.

- Marji was supposed to be your date for your graduation prom but she got sick and couldn't go. You took Barbara Anne instead and soon the two of you will celebrate your 15th wedding anniversary.

- Ormstead's Hardware Store decided to interview the summer job applicants in alphabetical order. You were the first interview, and you got the job. Ten years later you bought out Mr. Ormstead. Now a millionaire, you have six store locations.

How can anyone take credit for any of these "turns in the road?" Were they all "just meant to be?" Does it matter if they "fit" or not? Is there supposed to be a specific life purpose against which we should weigh the relevancy of such events?

If my parents hadn't skimped to send me to a small private high school after I failed two consecutive grades, I'd have been sent off to vocational school. Absolutely nothing wrong with that, but, instead of working as an auto mechanic, I became a psychologist and developed an interest in the things you are reading about. And if I hadn't written this book, you'd be doing something else right now.

Back in the early '70s, if my friend Fred Romanuk hadn't needed more people to form a "T-group" for an experiment he was doing in graduate school, I would not have discovered a knack for leading groups. Toward the end of my undergraduate work in psychology, I applied for a management job in a psychiatric institution. They liked me, but the qualifications required at least a completed BA and I didn't have one yet. For the next two months they hemmed and hawed and finally offered me the job. It was the week after I had decided to start my own training and consulting business instead. Thank goodness for bureaucratic indecision!

My wife Georgia and I met when my bank manager took me to her country line-dancing class. There she introduced me to Georgia and we discovered that her brother and I had both been fellow remedial students in the same small private high school. Georgia invited me to his 50th birthday party and we haven't been apart since.

I've still got to marvel: Who put all of these 'coincidences' together like that? Do you ever look back and marvel at the twists and turns of your own life? I don't think many of us marvel unless we've been through something rare and dramatic. If our car was crushed flat and we got out with only a scratch, we might marvel. If we inherit a castle in Scotland from an ancient relative we've never heard of, we might marvel. It's *marvel*-ous if we discover that a brother, separated from the family at birth, is living just a block away. However – and this may hurt a little – the truth is that not only do we not marvel about our own life, most others don't much care about the miracle of our life either. Like the forest hidden behind the trees, the universe is so miraculous that we don't see the miracles. On the other hand, we can be comforted by the good news that that doesn't make our lives any less of a miracle.

As much as I humbly and gratefully attribute the course of my life to the wisdom, love and patience of God, in no way do I see life as a ride where all we have to do is pull down the safety bar and hang on. One of God's greatest gifts is that he has asked us to help him finish the creation that he began. Our lives are as grand a part of creation as the separation of night from day and land from sea. Our choices, desires and yearnings are all part of this creation and are as real in their potential as anything that exists. The point many forget or deny is that we are *co*-creators with God. *We* have a responsible role to play in fulfilling the desires of our own heart. God is not a "drive-through" where a mysterious voice says, "May I take your order please?" That wouldn't be much of a partnership, would it?

In his book *Gravitation*, physicist John Wheeler poses the intriguing question, "May the universe, in some strange sense, be brought into being by the participation of those who participate?" For him the answer is "Yes," and he goes on to conclude that indeed, the vital act of life is the act of participation. There is no reality that comes from "out there" and smacks you like a cream pie in the face. There is no "arms-length" in life or a one-way mirror. There is no such thing as a life "observer." For example, I could not simply *observe* you reading. In trying to do so, I would alter your experience of reading and you would alter my experience of observing to the point where we'd end up creating a totally new reality for us both.

Think about this. You spend two hours in a totally useless meeting. People play political games, withhold the truth, and don't express their real thoughts and feelings. What a total waste of time! Time is a non-renewable resource and you've just thrown away a chunk of it. You walk out into the hall muttering to yourself and run into John Wheeler. "What a useless and dishonest meeting," you complain. "No it wasn't," he'd chide. "*You* participated in it uselessly and dishonestly." He'd have a good point. After all, you didn't put up your hand and speak the truth, did you? You didn't say what was really in your heart, did you? How can you talk about that meeting as though it happened beyond you? When did you suddenly become so impotent and helpless? *You* were part of participating that miserable experience into existence.

Of course, it works the other way too. The meeting can be amazing if honest connections are made among the participants. Wisdom can flow from all sources and powerful decisions can be made. If you met John Wheeler and told him what a wonderful experience that was for you and the entire team, he'd say. "Congratulations. You participated amazingly!"

Know it or not, admit it or not, you and I are constantly participating reality into existence. Now here is the part that amazes and confuses me at the same time. So please, humor me and accept that we are participating *a* reality into existence. Now exactly *what* reality is that?

If we are, indeed, co-creators of reality with God, that would seem to imply that God had not really finished creation when he stopped to rest on the seventh day or he would have no need of us. Maybe he finished just what he wanted to do on his own. An interesting notion is that God took all of the unfinished creative work left to do in order to bring every aspect of this universe to complete fulfillment, and divided it up among all the people who have been and will be born. I have a piece of it and so do you. So did Moses, Socrates, George Washington, Ghandi, Amelia Erhardt, and your late grandmother. Babies who will be born this year already have their assignments. What an awesome act of strategic planning this is, even for God. Most managers go crazy just trying to schedule people's vacations. Now let's push this thinking even further. What if our creative "assignments" were divinely chosen so wisely, with such supernatural foresight, and with such love that they somehow turned out to match, or parallel, the desires of our hearts? In other words, is it possible that our secret passions are already planted within us even though we may not have consciously clarified or expressed them yet? Is what we are participating into existence automatically, by definition, what we want? Are we already doing it?

If your life is in the pits right now, your immediate reaction will be, "I sure hope not!" Entertain this other notion for just a moment. Maybe, just maybe, we all have an actual divine purpose! In his amazing book, *Seat of the Soul,* author Gary Zukav shares this insight: "Before it incarnates, each soul enters into a sacred contract with the Universe to accomplish certain things. It enters into this commitment in the fullness of its being. Whatever the task that your soul has agreed to, all of the experiences of your life serve to awaken within you the memory of that contract, and to prepare you to fulfill it." Some of us see this contract as being with a personal God rather than with the more ubiquitous "Universe," but that does not lessen the power of his insight. Our souls have agreed to fulfill certain tasks and every experience we have is meant to jog our memory of that agreement.

The idea that you are participating goodness and prosperity because these outcomes are all part of a God-given "assignment" is very reassuring. But, if you are participating in poverty is that because somewhere deep inside you really want poverty and that God's "assignment" requires it? Mother Teresa probably would have said, "Yes – exactly!" Those of us a little less saintly are not so quick to respond that way. This is tricky territory so let's bravely explore it.

To paraphrase an ancient proverb from the Bible, "As a person thinks in his heart, so is his participation." It is this premise that makes this exploration perilous. What if a person is participating in an unkind, hurtful, vengeful or even evil way? Is the tragic and damaging outcome of his participation truly reflective of what he wants? Frankly, I think so. It must fulfill some purpose or he would do something else. Why he wants such outcomes, I can barely begin to guess (though I'll share some insights later). I believe we are all participating our desired reality into existence.

Now here is the conundrum. 1) Does this mean that, if I am having a really negative and painful reality right now, that I participated my own misery into existence? It may be true that "we reap what we sow," *but* do we always "sow what we reap?" 2) If my "wants," the desires of my heart, are already within me, am I able to change those desires and thus make the outcome of my participation more positive, rewarding and pleasant? Can people – can I – really change systemically?

The first problem is usually a tough one, though sometimes it can be answered quite easily. Let's say a person chooses to drink too much, participates in driving himself home and in wrapping his car around a tree. If he survives, I'd have to say, "Buddy, you participated your reality into existence." (If this happened in the US, he'd probably sue the company that planted the tree.) Still the big question is this: *Did drinking, driving and running into a tree reflect this man's deep "wants," the desires of his heart?*

Could the same be true of an imprisoned man who states that his wife drives him crazy and that's why he beats her? Incredulously, we shake our heads at his anger and irrational "reality." I don't have any hesitation with this scenario either. *He* participated his incarceration into reality. But again: *Is he fulfilling what he really wants?*

And what about the high school student who exclaims, "I just can't do it!" when asked to explain how he got 36% on his chemistry exam. "It's a stupid subject, and no one likes the teacher," he complains. "You can't even understand what she's saying half the time!" (Okay on this one I slow down a little because I *did* get that grade back in high school. I remember it because the teacher announced it in front of the whole class.) *Maybe he actually can't do it and if so how can we hold him responsible for this participation? Would you conclude that he actually **wanted** to fail chemistry?*

Some of us who were academically challenged were accused of just that by exasperated parents who had exhausted every technique they knew to get us to perform. "Sometimes I think you actually *want* to fail!" is how I think the line went, mixed occasionally with, "Do you *want* to spend the rest of your life in grade ten?"

And think about a manager with a fetish for emotional control who abuses the people who report to her. Overly directive, she allows virtually no opportunity for creativity and there are dark stories of what happens when people actually take risks and show initiative. When her department scores the lowest in employee satisfaction in the company's annual survey and their productivity drops a full 18% below the previous year, she responds with even more demands and tighter control. Well, I believe that people serve the way they are managed. If treated with disdain, they will do their work and serve their customers the same way. *Do you think she participated those results into existence and, if she did, why on earth would she actually "want" results like those?*

At first glance, these seem to be simple examples of how we do indeed participate our reality into existence, regardless of how pleasant or unpleasant that reality may be. Gary Zukav has a terrific insight on this point, too. He writes, "Every action, thought, and feeling is motivated by an intention, and that intention is a cause that exists as one with an effect. If we participate in the cause, it is not possible for us not to participate in the effect. In this most profound way, we are held responsible for our every action, thought and feeling, which is to say, our intention." **So our intentions, the wants and desires of our hearts, give direction to our participation which, in turn, creates our reality.** True enough. However, store this conclusion as a sub-total in your mind because we have to add up some other things before this all comes together. We'd be on very fragile ground if we were to stop here on our climb toward the *Seven Secrets.*

Even with the almost "unarguable" examples already noted, we have to at least entertain the idea that, just maybe, some other factor or person shared in the participation of those realities. In the courts, drinking establishments have been held responsible for continuing to serve someone obviously intoxicated and then failing to prevent that person from driving. And is there any chance that the abusive man had some kind of chemical imbalance that made him so violent? Or, even more likely, maybe he was raised in an abusive family himself and we should hold his parents at least partly responsible for his current behavior. If there was a learning disability limiting that high school student, how can we say his poor results were all because of him? Maybe he did have a lousy teacher. What if the company that the manager works for refuses to pay people adequately, forcing the manager into hiring poorly trained people? What's she supposed to do? Or maybe her boss is equally demanding and she's just passing it on.

Still, these examples are relatively trivial, so let's move on to some really tough cases. I have several friends engaged in a war against cancer. They are good, caring and wonderful people. They don't smoke, they eat wisely and do a reasonable amount of exercise. You won't catch me telling them that they participated their cancer into existence, I'll tell you that! And I'd have very little patience with anyone who did. They didn't "want" cancer. How could somebody *want* a disease? If they'd been smoking two packs of cigarettes a day for twenty-seven years, there would be room for discussion, but that isn't the case. Yet at the same time all of us have to join together in admitting that we participated in creating a world filled with environmental pollution and prolific use of chemicals and toxins linked to cancer. From our behavior, maybe some of us *do* want a disease.

There was a very sad situation involving the Canadian Red Cross and its control of the national blood supply. HIV tainted blood was allowed to get into the system and unsuspecting people were contaminated. They didn't participate that occurrence into existence either. They trusted the health care system and, in many cases, ended up being condemned to death. They didn't have careless sex or share needles with drug addicts in some dark alley.

In sad and unfortunate realities such as these, there are no thoughts of condemnation or judgment because we see these people as victims of circumstances created through the irresponsible participation of others. So how do we reconcile these situations with our sub-conclusion that we all participate our realities into existence? What did their intentions have to do with the effect on their lives?

The bottom line is this: **No one participates alone**, not even if we want to. All of our various participations are influencing one another, be it for good or ill. The proverbial flap of the butterfly's wings does influence El Nin~o. Martin Luther King Jr. once said that, "We are all caught in an inescapable network of mutuality." Are we ever! We *are* "our brother's keeper." There isn't even an option to be otherwise. Our participation influences all other participations just like a drop of water raises the level of the entire ocean.

It is difficult to admit this, but sometimes how I have participated reality into existence has been hurtful to others participating their reality into existence. The biggest regret of my life is, and will always be, how often in years past I chose to travel to some conference, or work in my office, instead of spending time with my children. I participated in absence and selfishness and that hindered them from participating in joy, confidence, and security. It does not seem fair that they have to live with the results of my participation as well as their own but that's the way it is. To give myself equal time, I'll add that I have also participated generously and lovingly with my children as well as with others. It is not a matter of needing "credit" for that positive participation. For me it is a matter of being able to look back at how I participated unselfishly and being glad that I did so. I believe it helped the recipients move their desired reality into existence, too.

Marriage, of course, is a situation in which two participations come together in a most intimate way. Sometimes the participations create something wonderful and sometimes they don't. In the "don't" case, we go out and look for someone else who just might be a better or more compatible participator. Unfortunately, in marriage many of us have spent a great deal of energy trying to get our partner to change how they participate while, foolishly and ironically, trying to insure that our own participation remains unchanged. The grand myth, of course, is that physically leaving an incompatible participator will actually remove the effect of that participation. Sorry, but that participator is going to be with you for the rest of your life, in one way or another.

Likewise, in business, managers try all the techniques they've learned in workshops to get the participation of their subordinates to change. But when the manager's own participation is left intact, or when the general corporate environment (think of it as a collective participation) remains without review, we cannot expect much to happen. There is no such thing as isolated change.

Here's an example. I recently took out more life insurance to cover the mortgage. The "sales process" involved my agent convincing me to change my participation as it pertained to the reality of my financial security. All sales, marketing and advertising ventures have that same objective: changing our behavior. The infamous infomercial works because we have a half-hour to watch others participating with a product on television. People just like us are participating with the juicer, the revolutionary make-up, the exercise machine and so on. We buy the stuff because we want to look like, be as healthy as, or just have as much fun as they do. We want to participate in life just like them. So much of life seems to be one participation against another participation, one self-interest against another self-interest.

Take something as basic as food. Some food producers add unpronounceable chemicals to their products, or spray them on their produce. You don't even want to know what goes into most hot dogs. If a company can get another two weeks of shelf life out of a product by adding a nitrate or a flavin or a glomerate, what do they care if it actually hurts you twenty years from now? Increased profit is the obvious goal. What is not so obvious is that these people are major participators in your life's reality.

This chapter is being written on a plane to Seattle. The pilot is a co-participator of mine. I truly hope he is happy and healthy. I'm going to help his participation by fastening my seat belt and turning off this computer when he tells me to. There is a big man in the middle seat next to me. We are playing the "who owns the armrest?" game. He is a co-participator too. One row behind me, a baby named Scott has been crying for a solid twenty-five minutes. This baby is now a co-participator with me. I hear his mom telling her seatmate her hopes that Scott will "participate" with the Seattle Mariners when he grows up. When we land, a man named Steve is going to meet me and take me to the conference location. I am already participating in his day and he in mine and I haven't even met him yet. My job and joy is to talk to a room full of other professional speakers about how to have a truly significant influence on their audiences. If I fulfill this responsibility well, at least one of them will have a greater impact on an audience somewhere than he would have had without me. Isn't this an amazing design, this universal, omni-present co-participation?

Yet, the aspect of this design with which I have the most difficulty pertains to the fact that many people suffer because of the participation of others. In Phoenix a mother inexplicably set fire to herself and her three children. As he lay dying in his older brother's arms, twelve-year-old Ramon asked "How could Mom do this to us?" In Jonesboro, Arkansas, two boys, eleven and thirteen years old, shot a teacher and several students dead after luring them outside with a false fire-alarm. In Littleton, Colorado, two students with semi-automatic handguns, shotguns and explosives conducted an assault on Columbine High School. Twelve students, one teacher and two suspects died. Twenty-four students were taken to local hospitals, some with life-threatening wounds. Six months later, another seventeen year-old Columbine student was expelled when he was found to have a twelve-page plan for "finishing the job." The same sort of thing happened in Fort Gibson, Oklahoma. Early in 2000, Arizona school officials were deeply concerned because over a dozen schools had received threats of a similar nature.

The Child Welfare League of America tells us that, out of the twenty-six richest countries in the world, 73% of all homicides against children happen in the United States. One in five teens regularly carries a gun, knife or club according to the Centers for Disease Control and Prevention. In 1996, almost 500 babies under one year of age died from abuse or neglect.

So many circumstances are so hard to understand. A family loses its home in a mud slide because the house was built too close to the bluffs. A young man is paralyzed because his friend drives recklessly. An aircraft crashes because of inadequate maintenance. There are other examples, not quite as visible. How about the businessman whose reputation is ruined because of a rumor circulated by a disgruntled employee? I know students whose four-year program was canceled by the college in year two. There is the builder left holding a year's worth of receivables because the contractor went bankrupt. How about those prisoners in Los Angeles who were wrongfully imprisoned because the "evidence" had been tampered with by police? None of these events are "fair."

We have all been recipients of unfairness. Just as in a business team, sometimes one of the team members lets everyone down and everyone suffers. But if we did not have this indigenous phenomenon of interdependency, the whole idea of "teamwork" would be foolishness. We are all in this together. We are participants in one universal team, like it or not. Other members of our team include dictators Saddam Hussein and Fidel Castro, Christian evangelist Rev. Billy Graham, comedian Jerry Seinfeld, billionaire techno-whiz Bill Gates, Playboy founder Hugh Hefner, President Bill Clinton and baby Scott, perhaps a future Seattle Mariner. Some of these team members we like and others we would be glad to be without. But no one has asked you or me to be in charge of team membership. Some of our team members, like Princess Di and Mother Teresa, are gone now and our team feels weaker without them. I'm just glad to know that you are on the team, too.

There are several points to all this.

a) We are each responsible for participating our own reality.

b) Countless other people and factors are also participating our reality.

c) Sometimes they do so with our good in mind and sometimes they do so out of their own self-interest and don't give a damn about our reality.

d) Sometimes we can influence the degree of impact these other co-participators have on our reality and sometimes we can't. (I can choose where I buy my vegetables but I can't choose the pilots on my flights.)

e) You and I are influencing other people's realities, too. Sometimes they are glad we are doing so and sometimes they wish we wouldn't.

f) There is no end to the impact our participation has throughout the world and, maybe even beyond, to worlds we don't even know about.

This last point reminds me of the AIDS warning we used to hear so frequently. "It's not just who you've slept with," the warning went, "it's who they've slept with, and who they've slept with, and who they've slept with..." When you let your frightened mind run with this thinking, you end up having slept with the entire world. If that didn't sober you up, I guess nothing would. In the same way, our participation's impact on other people's participation literally has no bounds. The whole universe reverberates with our participation. My understanding is that the origin of AIDS in North America can be traced back to a flight attendant. It is hard to imagine just how much his choices and behavior have influenced reality. Likewise, for good or ill, you and I are helping to participate the entire world's reality as well, and that should sober us up even more.

A short ways back, I mentioned the word "omni-present." This word is about as ungraspable as you can get. I first came to know about omnipresence back when I was studying theology. As you might expect, it was applied to God's omnipresent quality. I couldn't resist looking in one of my old systematic theology texts as a refresher. In 1907, Augustus Hopkins Strong, theologian and president of Rochester Theological Seminary, wrote, "God, in the totality of his essence, without diffusion or expansion, multiplication or division, penetrates and fills the universe in all its parts." (We used very old books in theology school, they made us feel much more ecclesiastical.) The truth of it all, however, is very current. At one and the same time, all of God is fully with my family members who live in Scottsdale, Vancouver, Toronto and Montreal. In addition, all of God is fully with me on this airplane and with you wherever you are. Don't ask me how *any* "being" can totally be everywhere at all times, but, if God can't do that, he doesn't get to be God anymore. When you watched Wayne "the Great One" Gretsky play hockey, you might have said, "He *is* all over the rink, he seems to be everywhere!" That isn't true. Only God *is* everywhere.

The aspect of omnipresence that really baffles me is that it is not time-bound. God is simultaneously in yesterday, today and tomorrow. There is no language for this because our language is time-language. It doesn't make sense for me to say, "At this *moment* God is in the *last century, this century* and the *next century.* All these italicized words are time-words and consequently they contradict the notion of omnipresence. We could say that God is omnipresent for "eternity." Most of us, however, think of eternity as a time-line that starts after we die. "Where will you spend eternity?" shouts the street-corner preacher at the passing crowds. I've got news for you – and him – you're spending it right now. Eternity, by definition, doesn't "start" anywhere. It always is. Like a circle, it has no beginning and no ending.

Do you ever think that the internet is a technological metaphor for the simultaneous, mystical and spiritual connection that we all have? A British artist by the amusing name of Paul Sermon insists that we have to accept the "omnipresence of the computer." There is even a web site development company called "Omnipresence." Because the entire world is linked technologically, we can instantly connect with many remote parts of the world "omnipresently." I think that is why God allowed us to discover the technology so we'd start to "get" the fact that we are all connected in a spiritual, omnipresent way. From God's point of view, the Internet, that so boggles our minds, is yesterday's news.

Is the impact of our participation linear and time-bound? Who knows? It may not have a *retroactive* impact in the sense that something we do today impacts on something that happened yesterday. Maybe it does and our minds just have not developed enough to understand a time-less dimension. I *do know* that our participation today impacts on the world's reality for centuries to come. We still feel the impact of the participation of Aristotle, Columbus, Lincoln, Michelangelo, Churchill, Shakespeare and countless others.

What we seldom stop to think about, however, is that all around these visible historical figures were thousands of their co-participators we know nothing about. People who, because of their now anonymous and seemingly minor participation, enabled world changers to do what they were meant to do. Who encouraged Aristotle to think differently than other little kids? Who first took the young Christopher Columbus to the seaside and pointed to the horizon? Who talked Lincoln into growing a beard? What were the names of the men who built the scaffold for Michelangelo to lie on while he painted the Sistine Chapel ceiling? Who brought him lunch? When did Churchill light his first cigar and who gave it to him? Who taught a young Will Shakespeare that the bump on the letter "q" goes that way and the bump on the letter "p" goes this way?

Likewise our participation may not make it to history books, but it is as potentially far reaching as that of anyone of notoriety. Study your personal and family history and you'll see what I mean about the impact of even minor acts of participation from those who have been part of your life. We would all behave so differently toward one another if we truly understood this. *Every* participation has consequences.

In Chapter Three, I will introduce you to Glenn Taylor. He taught me Psychology 101. One introductory course in college, that's it. And he changed my life. Dr. Ray Daly taught me one course and Dr. Marvin Kaplan taught me two courses. They changed my life too. Dorothy Kamp gave me a part-time job as a hospital orderly when I was in my twenties. Now I have consulted or spoken to over 200 health care organizations around the world. The meaning-filled life is usually built with very small participations.

Finally, it's vitally important to remember that your life's participation is not just about *you*. It's about everyone else on the planet, too. Generally, we have been very self-centered and angry participators. "Nearly 1.3 billion people live on less than a dollar a day, and close to 1 billion cannot meet their basic consumption requirements," declares the 1999 Human Development Report from the United Nations. Our anger and self-centeredness is why the world has so many homeless and why we keep having wars. That's why people divorce each other and why the most dangerous highway problem is "road rage." That's why young boys shoot-up their classmates and why the Republicans and Democrats spend billions of taxpayer dollars fighting each other. That's why auto manufacturers have to recall hundreds of thousands of cars for safety reasons and why America is so unbelievably litigious.

Ever find yourself responding even to those you dearly love in an unkind and critical way? Me too. We can actually "hear" ourselves sounding so awful and yet we still do it. We walk away from the situation smacking ourselves on the head because we are ashamed. Do any of these scenarios ring true?

- Your sister-in-law almost goes to the extreme of wearing her clothes inside-out just so you'll see the designer labels. You get your clothes at Wal-Mart and then only when they're on sale. All during the drive to her house for dinner you keep saying to yourself, "I'm not going to let her get to me, I'm not going to let her get to me, I'm not going to let her get to me…" You don't even have your coat off and she has mentioned Calvin Klein three times, like he's coming over. You lose it, and everyone suffers through a miserable evening. You end up feeling like a jerk.

21

- Bracing for the manager's strategic planning meeting, you still feel the sting from last year's session. No more! No sir! Let some other department take all the hits this time. Forget this "team" crap. You're tired of explaining to your staff why you have to downsize when no one else seems to. This time you are going to speak up, stand firm, insist on what's fair, hold your own! The President doesn't even take a seat as he begins, "This won't take long. Let me outline the restructuring plan that has been approved by the Chairman …" You end up with the short end of the stick again! Way to speak up, Tiger. Hate your own cowardice don't you? Wimp.

- The customer who accounts for 23% of all your company's sales has just informed you that he is going to re-tender the contract after seven years. The reason? He doesn't feel that you "want" the business anymore. You've gotten too smug he says. You no longer hustle and go the extra mile. You're complacent. Shocker huh? The trouble from your perspective is that you didn't even *know* you were participating complacency. You actually told the customer he was wrong about thinking you didn't care about his needs. How on earth did this happen to you and can you change it?

- Your drinking has been the source of more than one battle. It's been the source of a ten-year-war. You have hurt people emotionally and twice even physically. When you sober up and see what you've done, you cry like a baby, say you're sorry and beg for forgiveness. The routine is two hours of self-

flagellation followed by a drink. And around you go
again. It's not a very merry-go-round, to say the least.

If we find ourselves participating in a way that puzzles
and annoys even us, can we come to understand why we
are doing that and then change it for the better? Or
should we blame God for planting those negative intentions within us in the first place? If you choose the latter,
you might as well give this book to someone else and milk
your negativity for all it's worth. My prayer is that you
won't choose this option.

So, can we change? Yes – but not until we understand
where our hurtful and negative intentions come from.
Understand that the world is an angry place. Angry people
working in angry organizations. Couples in angry marriages. Angry teachers teaching angry children. Angry
policemen patrolling streets looking for angry criminals.
Angry sales people selling stuff made by angry manufacturers to angry customers. Angry national leaders trying
to out-maneuver other angry national leaders. I dislike
seeing myself writing angrily like this. I believe that, right
now, anger is the energizing emotional fuel of choice and
it's making us much less than ideal participators in every
aspect of our lives.

In *Going Deep,* I made the case for seeing anger as a
divine source of energy. Anger can, potentially, lead us to
new insights about who we are, who God is, and what we
are meant to accomplish through our lives. In short, make
us better participators. I believe this more than ever and
in the next two chapters I will dig even deeper into what
this anger is all about and how we can turn ourselves
around from it.

What Is the Meaning and Purpose of My Life?

You can find the answer to the most difficult question in the universe.

ACTION ONE

Don't be afraid to wander around in this big question for a while. What does "meaning" mean to you? Mull on the idea of having a divine destiny. Does that excite you or do you think it's nonsense? Be clear about what it is you are really trying to answer. Then you will be ready to move on.

Remember: you cannot create a life of meaning by yourself. Other people, your "co-participators," have been put into your life, some to help you and some to distract you. Remember what your Grandmother used to say? "You are known by the company you keep." Maybe your parents used to worry that you were "hanging out with the wrong crowd." Both of these expressions are right. You can associate with the co-participators who are here to help you or you can associate with co-participators who will keep you from finding meaning and destiny.

Think of who might be in your life that you know, in your heart of hearts, is *hindering* the discovery of your destiny. This is more difficult to do than you might initially think because some of these people may be very close to you. You may love them and they may love you, but they are still in the way. An over-protective mother can keep

24

you from your destiny. There may be enormous pressure from the whole family for you to take over the family taxidermy business when the very thought of it makes you sick. A chauvinistic spouse can emotionally and spiritually imprison you, ensuring that you do not become the person you are meant to be.

Some "self-help" books will tell you to disassociate yourself from people who seem to be such hindrances. They will tell you to cast them out of your life! But let's get real here. You can't run people out of your life just because they present an obstacle to you. If it's your mother, what are you going to do, tell her she has to go? Frankly, life would be quite boring without obstacles every once in a while. These people are like the wind that forces the tree to set down deeper roots. Their attempts to shake you from your divine purpose will cause you to take an even tighter grip! The absolutely critical lesson here is to keep on loving them *but get yourself back in charge of your own life!* Live your life under your *own* choices, *not* the choices of others.

Here is the other side of such situations. If you are associating with people living shallow, pointless and maybe even evil lives, you just may need to do something a little more drastic and indeed get them out of your life. If these people keep going the way they are going, they will never find meaning or destiny in their lives and, worse, they will be determined that you won't either. *They've got to go and you know it!*

Your Assignment

1) Make a list of the co-participators who are hindering you from finding your answer. Beside each one put either "can stay" or "has to go." With those who are "staying," start

to take charge of your own life. Keep loving them, keep your sense of humor and, above all, remember that they have a vital role to play, if only to test your determination to discover your own answer. As far as those that "have to go" are concerned, I think you know what you need to do. Do it *without* judgment and *with* kindness and courage.

2) Make a second list that identifies those co-participators who are able to provide you with wisdom, perspective, guidance, challenge and feedback as you seek your answer. These are the people you need to spend more time with. Ask them questions. Find out how they've made key decisions in their lives. Pursue these people rather than wait for them to come to you or for a chance meeting at some cocktail party. Life is a buffet, not a sit-down meal! No one is going to serve you. You've got to walk up there and fill up your own plate.

3) Keep your mind and heart open for the *new* co-participators who are about to come into your life, because they surely will if you are open to them. Once you create this consciousness, you will attract them to you. Did you meet someone yesterday and there just seemed to be a reason for your lives to connect? Well for gosh sakes, find out what the reason is. Try, with some frequency, to go through your day as though you are in an airport to meet someone you have never met before. Suddenly you see each other and you'll both know this is the connection you've been waiting for. Seek those who *know* the answer. You will know them because you will feel a connection, a co-participation of your spirits. This is an amazing and wonderful thing requiring only your intention to make it so.

Chapter Two

YOUR INNER JOURNEY

As I have tried to get a grip on my own life, a number of life-saving discoveries have come to me. One of those discoveries has to do with why anger is so much a part of our lives and how it can actually point us toward our destiny. That, for me, is a true, life-saving discovery. Still, I enter this chapter with caution because these new understandings and insights may not help explain *your* reality in the same way they have illuminated mine. I would never presume that they would, though I hope and pray you will discover your own "Ahas!" in what I am about to convey. When other speakers and authors try to convince me that they have found "my way" for me, I get nervous. "Look no further," they seem to say, "luckily I have found your answer for you." We all need the insights and teachings of others, but ultimately I want to find truth for myself, so that it is truly mine. So my purpose is only to set the table. Eat what you will.

Every individual is on a journey. Of course, your journey is a different color and shape than mine, and it has its own background music. You go up while I go down. You turn left when I swerve right. And since we are co-participators, both of our journeys are essential parts of one grand masterpiece. Regardless of what joys and pains we have experienced along the way, all that we bring to this discussion is beautiful.

My spiritual journey has been difficult. There were times when I didn't feel at all spiritual. Nevertheless, I have come to recognize "Six Spiritual Stations" at which I have stopped, sometimes repeatedly, on the way to finding and fulfilling my ultimate reality, my "creative assignment." Let me be clear that I am still on the way, and what you will be reading is what I have come to understand so far. (Should I have the joy of writing another book a year or two from now, I hope that I will be able to describe the inner journey more completely and insightfully.)

The Six Stations of the inner journey are spiritual conditions or experiences that we grow *through.* Each has its own unique characteristics and contributions and each is critical to our quest of understanding the "Whys?" of our lives. I have also come to recognize that our businesses and corporations are likewise on a spiritual and creative journey. Part of a grand design, they visit these same Six Stations. Corporations have a spiritual life that can either be led into atrophy and waste or into strength and significance. Because a corporation is nothing beyond a collective of spiritual beings sharing a common purpose, it *does* have a soul of its own. Think of it as Soul Inc. This corporate soul doesn't just sit there waiting for the excitement of the annual meeting; it wants to fulfill its "contract with the universe." That means each business entity has a spiritual purpose as divine in its origin as what drove Martin Luther to lead the reformation of the early church, Mother Teresa to bring comfort and hope to the destitute of Calcutta and Rev. Billy Graham to preach the message of the Gospel to millions around the world.

Does this mean that all corporations *act* in a spiritually responsible way? Obviously not. Corporations wander off their right path just like you and I do. And, like you and I, they are given signals by the universe that they are compromising their divine intention. Unfortunately, many corporate leaders are not exactly receptive to such notions and it is that vacuum that draws me into the work that I do. What I find at odds with leadership resistance to working with corporate spirituality is that companies will pay fortunes to consultants to help them develop a statement of "*mission*." I suggest to you that at some deep level we *know* there is a corporate spiritual life and a profound *purpose* behind our strategies, systems and structures. We who lead are responsible for the delineation and broadcast of this purpose. It is just too bad that there are so few resources to help leaders fulfill that responsibility.

These Six Stations, visited by individuals and corporations alike, are described in considerable detail in *Going Deep*. In that book I make a dual and simultaneous application of the Six Stations. One application is made to our personal lives and the other to our corporate or work lives. I do not see the value in separating the two, given that most of us who work outside of our homes spend more time with our employers than we do with our children. Our work institutions consume more of our time than any other institution in which we are involved. So I will maintain the dual application here too. The truths we will uncover are applicable to both. Because we need to make use of the Six Stations as a foundation, I want to present a condensed version of those insights and then move into new territory.

The first Station is called **INNOCENCE**. Here all of life seems fair. You believe that your co-participators care about you and would not do anything to hurt you. The infant expects to be fed when she is hungry and changed when she is wet. As an adult, you naturally trust others and are hurt and puzzled when someone tells you to get all the agreements of your life "in writing." Why? Because you take people at their word and operate on a philosophy of universal goodness. Your initial belief is that you can always trust your doctor, your kid's teachers, the police, your priest, pastor or rabbi, your nanny, your senator and the man who conducts the boy's choir. How wonderful life would be if it were so. The hurt, wounded and betrayed who left this Station long ago will look at you condescendingly and, at best, call you naïve or, at worst, foolish.

In its corporate manifestation, the Innocence Station is filled with excitement about new ventures and visions of sugar plums. Those who give birth to a new business are filled with such idealism and passion they often go for years without paying themselves for all their labor. The difference between "self-employment" and "unemployment" is hard to defend at the Innocence Station. You are so "into it" that you would, and do, work for free. Your work is your life and your life is your work. Every co-participator involved in the venture works in synchronization without thought of structure, turf or job description. You frame the first dollar or check you receive, the corporate version of the birth certificate. This is a grand place, indeed. All of us who have ever started a business reflect in fondness for those wonderfully difficult "early days." Most of the time we wonder where we ever got the nerve to do what we did. But we acted in simple faith and trust that our dreams could become a reality.

You don't have to be a full-fledged entrepreneur to feel this innocent exuberation. Most of us arrive at our new job, particularly if it is our first one, with an eagerness that knows no bounds. We'll help anywhere, stay late and wonder why people bother to take lunch when there is so much to do. This eagerness can begin to annoy the more seasoned employees who may do only the minimal demanded of them. You, in your industrious innocence, come bouncing in early on a rainy, dull, cold Monday morning bubbling, "Good morning everyone, let's serve somebody!" For sure that will identify you as a new employee. And if you have a natural zest for life you can probably maintain this enthusiasm in a typical bureaucracy for – oh, say – a week or two.

I facilitated a very senior-level conference a year ago and in trying to put a human touch on the series of "talking heads," I asked each presenter to tell the audience about his or her very first job. Every one of these austere and sophisticated executives, prepared to read yet another neutered corporate speech, suddenly lit up. We heard stories about carrying bricks, bagging groceries, cleaning boats and so on. Why the impromptu animation and joy? It was all because, just for a moment, they went back to the Innocence Station. There is a joyful purity about innocence. It is a wonderful and refreshing place to visit. Unfortunately, our world doesn't allow us to live there.

Try it for yourself. Think back to the innocent 'firsts' of your life. Your first pet. Your first car. Your first date. Your first kiss. Your first house. Unless something tragic is associated with these events, most of you will find yourself smiling at the recollection. Start talking to someone about your first car and you'll find yourself in an animated and happy discussion in no time.

Sadly, innocence does not last long; it comes to a crashing halt when you meet the first co-participator who is out to get you. The end can come with violence such as sexual abuse or abandonment. Sometimes it ends more quietly with experiences such as being teased at school, being criticized unfairly by a neighbor or being rejected by your first love. What these signals mean is that you'd better start looking out for yourself. You start to value the differences between yourself and the rest of the world and deliberately begin to separate yourself from other participators, particularly the ones you are beginning to dislike and distrust.

This second Station is called **INDEPENDENCE.** It is a shock at first, but soon the quest to find your Self, who you really are, starts to energize you. The major value of having six earrings in one ear is that your parents hate them. You definitely don't want to mimic their fashion sense even though *they* think their look is right and normal. Then, moving into your own apartment is the "twenty-one gun salute" of Independence. You didn't know it at the time, but it was probably your parents firing the guns. *Your* way of doing things, *your* personality, *your* choices, *your* behavior – these became the important things. Literally every aspect of your personal life became a metaphor for independence, from your messy bedroom to the tattoo your parents still don't know about, to your backpacking trip to Europe. It was all about finding You.

Some people, unfortunately, get stuck at the Independence Station. They become "loners," don't really belong to anything and, most unfortunately, seldom have real friends in their lives. They forget that we were not created to be alone and independent. Independence was never intended to be a terminal state. It is just a phase of growth in which we can gain enormous strength and identity. As we will see in a moment, the real goal is *interdependence*, or, as I have labeled it, *Integration*. There is not a lot of value in "discovering yourself" only to find that you are alone. We "find ourselves" only in the context of relationships with our co-participators.

The corporate version of Independence coincides with that incredible moment when you know your new business is going to work. You can actually take money out of the company! You get your first referral from one of your customers, the sure sign that this tree has taken root. A little cockiness starts to show itself as you berate your competitor's product, and have visions of how you are going to dominate the global marketplace someday. Something about "kicking butt" is how you put it. Great pride is taken in the fact that you violate convention. You are one of the "new breed," an up-and-comer, a rising star. You even pay to be included in one of those "Who's Who" directories along with 99,000 others trying to find their place in the sun.

One of the more foolish things that often happens at this Station is that you ignore or outright reject the wisdom of the ages, particularly the warning that selfishness and ego are traps from which it is very hard to escape. Often, you don't see a problem until it's too late. The euphoria of a new day, the dawn of a new age, indeed your own self-importance blurs your thinking. The logo your secretary drew is no longer good enough and so thousands are spent to have a graphics company draw almost the same thing. The office overhead you took on was way out of proportion to your revenue. You leased the Benz three years before you should have. All these decisions are part of identifying your Corporate Self to your Self and the marketplace. All are very essential to growth, regardless of how wise or foolish they may be.

The Independence initiative just starts to pay off for you when something happens. You won't know its impact for some time, but at the third Station, *INSTITUTION*, you are slowly drawn into the realization that there are participators out there who are bigger, stronger, smarter, richer, more authoritative and more powerful than you are. What happens is that you end up in institutions like family, school, religion and work. You may not recognize it at the time, but these institutions are forcing their brand of unity on you. In these places are people who get to tell you what to look like, how to behave, what and when to eat, what and when to pray, when to come to work and when to go home.

Finding yourself in these institutions is no surprise since it's just part of growing up. Literally everybody you know is in a multitude of institutions. You can't escape it, and frankly, you don't want to, at least not at first. As a matter of fact, there is considerable comfort in institutional routine and control. As far as I am concerned, the more rules the better when it comes to airline safety. And our entire legal system is based on institutionalized control. How else could it work? Wouldn't baseball look silly if you could run the bases in any order you considered advantageous at the moment? At first glance *institutionalization* seems to be the preferred way to organize our lives.

One hotel chain used to advertise that there were never any "surprises" when you stayed with them. That was because they had *institutionalized* their chain so the same architecture, color combinations, menus, pictures on the walls, and, most importantly, the same plastic plants appeared everywhere. It didn't matter if the hotel was in Alaska or Aruba, they were pressed from the same institutional mold. Likewise, two fast-food chains were put in clear juxtaposition when one of them came out with the slogan "Have it your way." The message was that their inflexible and institutionalized competitor forced you to eat the food the way *they* wanted you to rather than give you choices. Arguably the greatest culinary example of institutional thinking is the classic scene in the movie *Five Easy Pieces* where Jack Nicholson tries to order some toast and has to order a toasted chicken salad sandwich (hold the lettuce and chicken) to get it.

We have come to expect the control of an institution and actually learn to move from one to another of them all through life. When a child moves into a new institution such as a new school, his parent will tell him, "It won't be long before *you'll get used to it.*" When we get a new job that requires quite different skills than our old one, we tell our friends that we are "*getting used to it.*" What usually happens is that our desires, ambitions, dreams, giftedness and so on, adapt and conform to almost any institution. Of course every once-in-a-while we find ourselves in a situation that we *just can't get used to* and the dissonance between our Self and the Institution becomes increasingly blatant.

Depending on how benevolent and flexible these institutions are in treating you, you may begin to feel enriched, valued, treasured, stretched, energized and fulfilled. *Or* you begin to feel boxed-in, devalued, subservient, sanitized, impotent, controlled, de-personalized and uniformed. Sadly, my observation is that many of our major institutions – family, school, religion and work – tend to have the latter effect. It is not that they have evil intentions, it's just that for them life does not exist without bureaucracy, power, structure, control and regimentation. So you, well on your way to being a one-of-a-kind artist, helping to finish creation itself, suddenly wake up to the fact that you are doing "paint-by-numbers." I once saw a Freudian typo that referred to "*pain*-by-numbers," which I think conveys the point even better. Sooner or later you begin to feel that your *Self* has been lost somewhere in the relentless, if somewhat subtle, institutional pressure to comply and conform.

35

This discovery can happen in grade two by the free-thinking child who discovers very early that she does not fit into a system where teachers have little option but to teach all thirty-two kids in their classroom in a way that fits the "average" aptitude.

Or it can happen to someone a week from retiring when he realizes how meaningless and empty his work life has been for the last thirty-seven years. Seconds after the tea and cake are gone at the retirement party, his employer is going "Next!" as he throws the empty watchcase into the wastebasket. It's even worse if the retiree learns that he won't be replaced. Contrary to popular opinion, not being replaced does not usually mean you were irreplaceable.

It can also happen in families where a father's most common refrain is, "As long as you are under *my* roof, you'll abide by *my* rules!" That father probably didn't have any *"my"* things as he grew up. And now that he's got some, nobody is going to take them away. (However, I want to restate that I am all for some degree of institutionalization in the home. Two of our adult children moved *back* into our home for a while and, believe me, we laid down some institutional rules.)

In religion, should you voice serious questions about the institutional dogma of your faith, you can be threatened with the loss of your immortal soul if you don't get yourself straightened out and start fitting in. But I must ask where on earth did we get the idea that God does not want us to question things? Can you imagine God conducting a Q & A session? "Any questions?" he'd ask and none of us would say anything. Sounds like most staff meetings. What a wasted opportunity that would be. In the religious institution in which I was raised, church was 100% predictable, only the hymn numbers changed and even that wasn't very often. There the Spirit of God couldn't be set free if it was wrapped in dynamite and the fuse was lit.

Now at some point, the questions we all have at the Institution Station are, "What happened to *me?*" and "Where did my emerging, creative Self go?" We are likely to ask that in the context of our family, school, religion and work. And, indeed, something *has* happened to us. Because it usually happens slowly and quietly, we don't fully understand it. A tension has crept up on us like the tide on a sleeping sunbather. We're not sure who the enemy is and we aren't sure how we'd fight back if we did know. All we *do* know is that we don't like it. Something has gone terribly wrong and an immobilizing fear begins to grip our lives.

You may question why I am describing this experience as horrific, especially if you have not experienced any trauma in your institutions. Maybe your family didn't abuse you, school was fine and, most importantly, the source of all your friendships. In university perhaps you couldn't understand why you had to take a course from column "C" because those courses had nothing to do with your career plans, but that was just fleeting frustration at most. There's a lot of politics and regimentation where you work, but aren't all companies pretty well the same? I mean, how many places do you know where all the employees are deliriously happy? You are generally committed to your faith and do your best to follow the tenants of your religion. So where is the big problem?

The fact is that institutions of all sorts have a reliance on structure and control. That is what makes an institution an institution. There is nothing fundamentally wrong with this *until that structure and control begins to minimize your uniqueness and removes from you those choices that you are perfectly capable of making.* In the family institution, for example, a wife may be kept in subservience by an unfeeling and dominant husband. Or an overly protective mother may treat her adolescent son as though he was still five years old. In school a student may be academically "punished" for failing mathematics while at the same time is given no encouragement to exercise an unusual musical gift. A graduate student may despair over the incredible intrusion of politics into academia. Real learning seems to be secondary to the bureaucratic wranglings of the administration. At work a man's job description is so detailed, so defining that he doesn't even have to think; all he has to do is look up the situation in a manual and be compliant. A simple expenditure of $100 requires three signatures. A woman who spent eight months developing a complex proposal is not allowed to present it because she has status deficiency. Her boss does, however, and takes all the credit. A gay man, devoted to his faith, is stunned by the cruelty, self-righteousness and lack of love on the part of other believers. Regardless of where it comes from, the Institution Station is all about control and power over your life.

Some will think this is the way it is supposed to be and resign themselves to it from the very beginning which is a dangerous and misleading position. Others take a more strategic approach and negotiate, manipulate or manage their way around their various institutional systems until they are in a position to control the institution rather than the other way around. Some of our wealthy business tycoons, men and women who have vowed never to be controlled by anyone ever again, are prime examples of this. Yet others flail against the institution, usually hurting themselves in the process of trying to hurt it. The janitor charged with stealing, the employee fired because she was "sick" every Monday and Friday for over three months, the assembly line worker whose bungling and inept attention to quality caused the line to be shut down for almost an entire shift – these are all examples of people fighting against being controlled by the institution. All of this behavior can be summed up in one word: *anger.*

So welcome to Station four, the ***IRRITATION*** Station. To get right to the point, I think most of the world is angry. Even those who don't know or won't admit that they are angry are angry. Recently I noticed a license plate on a van that read IMMAD 2. At least that guy wasn't hesitant to let others know just where he was in his life. He is not alone. In major U. S. cities, as high as thirteen of every 100,000 deaths is due to road rage. Nowadays, air-rage incidents are being reported like any other violent events. There were ninety reported major instances in 1995 while in 2000 we are on track for 500, according to the Federal Aviation Administration. *Frequent Flyer* magazine found that four out of ten business travelers had witnessed air rage. On one flight, a disturbed teenage passenger who tried to break into the cockpit, died after other passengers attacked him.

I live in Arizona where, according to the Department of Public Safety, five to seven percent of people always carry a gun in their cars; 75% of them are loaded. We are three times more likely to end up in court than in a hospital according to the National Center for State Courts. And the American Bar Association claims, "More than half of all American households have a legal issue right now." Beyond the North American borders anger flourishes as well. In Sierra Leone, children are war veterans by eleven years of age. One of these kids was quoted as saying, "When someone moves, I just shoot." Foreign Aid groups estimate that between five and ten thousand children have been forced to fight in that country's civil war.

Anger, or irritation, is the result of the conflict between our quest for Independence and our compliance with our Institutions. We need to ask ourselves, "Are the institutions of our lives – marriages, schools, religions, work places – truly enabling us to become more of who we are meant to become?" If you were to phone me and tell me sincerely that, "Yes, they are!" I'd be thrilled. Some of mine are too, particularly my marriage. However, you can pick almost any data source and you'll find that half of marriages don't work out. Three quarters of all employees do not see their jobs as a source of fulfillment. Many churches are struggling just to hang on to members. Schools are constantly being criticized because they don't seem to be preparing students adequately, and our children are in enormous struggles every day of their lives.

Of course there are exceptions and we desperately need them because they are our source of hope. But folks, look at the big picture. Some time ago, a Presbyterian newsletter ran an article on the "price of evil." Never mind "mad money;" look at where *angry* money comes from. Organized crime, 500 billion dollars. Drug traffic accounts for $150 billion along with 2,000 billion dollars from financial crime. Pornography is a $20 billion industry. Fraud kicks in another $300 billion. Gambling, sponsored by many governments, is doing well at $700 billion. We cheat on taxes to the tune of $180 billion. A simple skill like shoplifting brings in $90 billion. Military spending is somewhere around $950 billion. The article didn't even say how much prostitution brings in. And there is no line item for tobacco either. Both of these industries hurt people too. Well over 30 % of the gross world product is spent on inducing pain. A total of $5.2 *trillion every year!* In contrast, that same source estimates that it would take only $520 billion to feed and shelter the entire world's poor for a year.

We *are* an angry world.

At a conference I attended, a discussion developed around the anger issue. One man said, "I was raised in a very strict and religious home and I am raising my children the same way. I don't think I'm angry." While I am in no position to judge whether he is angry or not, my mind went back to all the years where I didn't think I was angry either. I had the same kind of upbringing he did and I know that part of the trap is that institutions are able to convince us there is a rule that says you can't get angry about the rules. This is a spiritual version of "Catch 22." Sooner or later, our anger at not being allowed to be angry gets the best of us.

But you know what? This is *not* a bad thing! Anger is a very necessary component of the spiritual journey, both personally and corporately. It is strange but true that the *Seven Secrets to a Life of Meaning* are just coming into focus at this stage. After all, not much would have happened in history without someone being irritated about something. Miraculous pharmaceuticals were developed because someone became irritated at a disease. Baby cribs were redesigned because someone got angry at the fact that babies were getting their heads caught between the bars and suffocating. Edison got tired of working in the dark. Ghandi was irritated at the way the British were treating his people. Every change you can think of was probably conceived in irritation. Irritation is the essential factor that turns gritty sand into smooth pearls. Irritation is the birth place of your meaning.

Recognizing that my anger was actually a divine source of energy was the most freeing discovery that I have ever made. The trick is to learn to use it for what it was intended. I believe that we are angry because we have not found our answer to the Universe's most difficult question. The purpose of your anger is to cause you to make choices for yourself, about what you believe, who you are, and what you will do. All anger points to a choice that is *not* being made or to a question not being answered. It is meant to lead you to your own insights about life, rather than to simply comply with the choices and insights dictated to you by an Institution. Sometimes in making choices for ourselves, we turn our backs on what we were force-fed at the Institutional Station, and end up choosing to believe something entirely different. Other times we reject an institutional belief and then, having worked through it for ourselves, choose that same belief again. This time, though, it is ours and that makes all the difference in the world.

As our anger prompts and enables us to make our own choices, we do so through the channel of **INSIGHT**, the fifth Station. Here we learn to see through all the institutional distortions of life to what *we* believe to be right, true and good, to what is important to our own becoming, to our divine assignment. We rejoice with each new discovery, laying insight upon insight until our lives are built into the temple they were meant to be, a testimony to God's creativity, creation coming to fulfillment. Here we find our truth. Here we are able to declare that we have found our meaning.

Many will argue that *their* truth is *the* truth and that any other insight is false. Frankly, I understand this, and to some degree, can be accused of the same stance. For example, I believe that God *is*, that he loves us, that he wants to have a personal relationship with us, that he intends for us to be co-participators with him. And, if you choose to, I'd like you to believe that too.

Still, not *all* our insights will match-up. We don't all have to end up in the same place around *every* issue. That sort of compliance is what the Institutions try to sell us. It is hard to put a boundary around Truth and measure its depth and breadth, and it is impossible to claim a monopoly on it. There is a glory to Truth that shines brighter than *ANY* Institution. Furthermore, the truth I have now is much more complete than the truth I had two years ago. Much of that growth has happened because my participation has changed. Two years from now it will have grown again. At least I am determined it will.

When I was in theology school, we would have stimulating, endless debates over various points of theology. Was there a difference between spirit and soul? Could Christ have sinned if he wanted to? Where do the souls of dead people go and how fast do they get there? Where exactly are heaven and hell? Because I was raised Baptist, I generally got the impression that Roman Catholics had really missed the boat with their insights. My psychology training, however, was at a Catholic university and I was exposed to Catholic priests as professors. I got to know them well. To my amazement I discovered that these men loved God, too. When I discussed this discovery with one of them he said sadly, "I understand. We were taught that you were wrong, too."

So where do I come down on all of this? Sometimes we insist on our truth to such a dogmatic degree and with such intensity that we are seen as taking away another person's choice. That is what most Institutions do, remember? Years ago I saw a cartoon of a crusader on a huge horse, his lance on the throat of a scrawny peasant lying on the ground. The peasant looks up and says, "Tell me about this Christianity of yours, I am terribly interested!" You can't arrive at truth without your own free choice. So to myself, and to you, my co-participator, I say, "Be gentle with your truth. When it is expressed with love, it will be attractive enough."

Finding truth or insight is difficult enough for us as individuals. However, that challenge is nothing compared to a corporation trying to find its truth. When a corporation is irritated, and in this post-re-engineered era most are, they don't think, "Our irritation is giving us an opportunity to gain new insights into the "why?" of our existence." When an institution gets angry it usually responds with more institutionalization, not more insight, somewhat like the notice on the bulletin board stating, "All social events are cancelled until morale improves." In other words, even *more* rules, structure and regulation are imposed. That, of course, makes people even angrier and the truth is pushed further and further away.

Regardless, there remains such a thing as corporate truth and it can only come from insight. What does your corporation really stand for? What does it believe in? What is the truth about the relationships within your workplace? What do you believe about serving others and about universal responsibility and accountability? Have you, together, really discovered the *meaning* of your work? Please notice that I didn't ask you about your corporate "values." Maybe I have become jaded over years of reading literally hundreds of so-called "Value Statements." Frankly, most of these do not reflect deep soul-searching. They haven't been conceived out of wrestling through the "whys?" of corporate existence and activity. They are the products of committees or consultants who were given the task of writing the corporate values in time for the annual meeting. I know of many such documents that were literally written by a public relations consultant. One CEO proudly showed me his company's Board-approved four-color poster titled "Our Values." "Good for you," I said. "Anytime people come together and commit themselves to what they truly believe in, there is cause to rejoice. Tell me how these values came to be." "What we did," he confided, "was write to several other 'best-practice' companies we admired and got a copy of their values. Then as a committee we decided which were the best ones."

Wouldn't it be wonderful instead if, every day, in our homes, schools, work-settings and places of worship, we could gather a new insight into the "whys?" of our lives? We can. As we gradually accumulate these insights and become more and more of whom we are meant to become, we enter the sixth Station, or **INTEGRATION**. This is where the various aspects of our participated reality start to line up and link with each other. We no longer regard the amazing connections of our lives as "coincidences." On the contrary, we regard them as normal. We *expect* them. Serendipity is a daily experience. We start to see the whole picture. The stuff of our lives makes sense.

Frankly, when good stuff happens to us, it is relatively easy to experience integration, the mystical connection and alignment between all things. I've read about a woman who won millions in a lottery by using the numbers her recently deceased mother had always played. How long, do you think, did it take that woman to come up with an explanation for how such an amazing thing happened to her? I guarantee she isn't pacing back and forth clutching at her head wondering, "Why did this happen to me?" She and her dead mother co-participated that reality. Are you going to convince her it was a fluke?

But what about when the "other" stuff happens? A fall broke your hip. Your university application was rejected. The luggage containing your great grandmother's diamond necklace was lost. You missed a fabulous investment opportunity by minutes. Your home was destroyed by a tornado. Your child suffers from a chronic ear-canal problem. These realities that hurt are much harder to integrate, like jamming your feet into much too small shoes. But even these occurrences at the Integration Station can lead to answers to the "whys?" if we allow them to do so.

It has only been in the last few years that I have really felt my life come together. Not completely, mind you, but just enough for me to believe that it can. There are still so many gaps in my own integration and, frankly, I don't care. Compared to the earlier part of my journey (I've been to hell and back so many times I could take tours) this is heaven. I am a happy and loved guy. Georgia and I have been married just over three years as I write this. Every once-in-a-while when we are curled up together, we muse on how we wish we had met when we were twenty-one instead of fifty-one and why we hadn't. We wouldn't have been the same Georgia or the same Ian who now love each other. Both of us had much more participating to do before this integration could happen. All of the participations that were part of our lives before we met are precious and have brought us to our current place. As I look back on all the times I wish I had participated differently, it is hard for me to just accept what was. Until we can accept what *was*, we'll never accept what *is*.

All of the vacuous initiatives we call management techniques are attempts to figure out "Why?" We put people through a battery of "personality" tests in order to figure out *why* they behave the way they do. We set up stringent processes for measuring quality in the hope that we can document *why* our products break down. We re-engineer and downsize in an effort to find *why* we aren't making as much money as we want. Many of these initiatives are poorly thought through, are demonstrations of institutional power, selfish in intention, and, I believe, conceived in anger. The questions we need to be asking ourselves within our organizations are not strategic, systematic or structural. They are *spiritual.* Until we recognize that, we will keep going from flavor of the month to flavor of the month. All the while we will continue to yearn for something we know is out there but can't quite grasp.

While chatting with one senior executive I asked, "What is it you yearn for, what goal do you see for this organization?" He was thoughtful for a moment and answered, "We want to hit the billion dollar mark." I said, "Why?" After another thoughtful pause, he replied with wonderful honesty, "I don't know." Frankly I think a billion was just the next big number. Where there is no answer to the question "Why?" there will always be restlessness. Maybe we ought to scrap the old Suggestion Box and put up a Why? Box.

Wouldn't it be wonderful if everyone, every team, department, supplier and especially customer were lined up behind one grand Why? There would be no energy lost in useless "make-work," no turf wars, nothing falling "through the cracks," no confusion over direction or strategy, no political power games. If you are a senior corporate leader, what would you give to unequivocally know that every single employee was right behind you 110%? Want to know what is preventing that from happening? Anger.

I believe we keep revisiting the Six Stations of the inner journey, depending on what our participation creates in our lives. The differentiating point between "breakdown" and "breakthrough" seems to be what we do at the Irritation Station. We are either destroyed by our angry participation, or we find a way to allow it to move us to a better and deeper place filled with insights and alignment. This is as true for individuals as it is true for organizations.

Given that the "make it or break it" point seems to happen at the Irritation Station, it is wise for us to come to a new understanding of why anger seems to be the emotion of choice in our families, schools, work, and even our places of worship. Once we understand irritation as an essential part of our development, we will be in a stronger position to lead others through it to a better place.

We are still climbing the mountain toward The Seven Secrets to a Life of Meaning. We have seen that this is not a journey we take alone. Many struggle with us – some help and guide, giving us a push or a pull just when we need it. Others, not so caring, push us toward a cliff or steal our rations. Our first choice, in the movement toward the Secrets, is to choose our climbing partners wisely.

We learned, too, that there are signposts along the way – spiritual signposts reassuring us that meaning lies somewhere ahead. Knowing there is a pattern to our journey does not make it any easier. We experience setbacks and confusion, often caused by those who want to control us and relegate us to compliance rather than release us to commitment. In a wonderfully ironic way, however, we are about to see that it is these very irritations and angers that announce the emergence of meaning.

What Is the Meaning and Purpose of My Life?

You can find the answer to the most difficult question in the universe.

ACTION TWO

Have you ever heard this kind of conversation? Usually it's about a couple who have just split up. "Why did they split up?" a person asks. "Well," someone explains, "she grew and changed over the years and he didn't." Of course the opposite could be true too, but you get the point. Some of us know that life is about growing and maturing. I believe that there may be more of a pattern to that growth than we think.

And if there is a pattern, it may be possible for us to know how we are doing if we measure ourselves against it. Your "assignment" then, begins with placing an imaginary "I am here" sticker somewhere on that pattern. Knowing just where you are comes before knowing where you are going.

After that you will be invited to review each of the "Stations" of the inner journey to see what personal truths you have been given. Just as when you log in and out of various websites you leave and accumulate "cookies," each time you are in one of these Stations you will be given a "cookie" of truth. Taking the time to review those learnings will be extremely helpful in your quest to answer the most difficult question in the universe.

Your Assignment

1) If you were to freeze-frame your life right now, where would you put your "I am here" sticker on this list?

Innocence

Independence

Institution

Irritation

Insight

Integration

If you had met me five or six years ago, my sticker would have been squarely on the Irritation line. As I write this, I would put it closer to Insight with occasional visits to Integration and some back to Irritation.

You can also put a sticker on the chart for your employer. At which Station does your company seem to be located right now? I speak to hundreds of corporations all over the world every year and I think about 90% of them are in the Irritation Station and wishing they could park in Institution so they could control everybody. Part of your job is to help your organization gain *insights* so it can move on in its own maturing instead of regressing into more institution.

I do not recommend you writing other people's names on the chart. Jotting, "Bob is here!" with a heavy arrow pointing to Irritation is not likely to lead to insightful discussion. *Think* that – just don't write it in the book and then leave it open on his desk.

2) This part of the assignment (on page 52) is more difficult than it looks and requires a lot of quiet reflection. Think back to your visits to these various stations and ask yourself what you learned from the experience. What truths have been given to you that may provide direction to your life? Don't spend your time "word-smithing" – just write words or phrases. You will know what they mean.

We've a long way to go, so do not concern yourself about coming to any conclusions. If we were playing poker, you'd be arranging the cards in your hand in order to see your options. On the next page are the "cards" you've been dealt. Now we will work toward doing something wonderful with them.

STATION	MY TRUTHS
Innocence (Think of situations where you had dreams and hopes and where you trusted others and felt that the world was a good and caring place.)	(Write the words/phrases that come to you)
Independence (Think of how you have tried to demonstrate your independence and what response you got when you tried to do it.)	
Institution (Think of your major institutions – family, school, work, religion – and how they have influenced you.)	A) Family B) School C) Work D) Religion
Irritation (Think of those periods of real restlessness you've had. What were they all about and what did you do with the restlessness? Is it still with you?)	
Insight (Think of those "break-throughs" in your life where you have come to see the world, and yourself, differently.)	
Integration (Think of those wonderful moments when you have truly known "Why?" Recall when life actually made sense, where you felt connected to others, to God and to your experiences in a very deep and spiritual way.)	

Chapter Three

USING YOUR ANGER AS A CATALYST FOR CHANGE

There are three natural experiences that seem to be on the same wavelength as the human heart: ***Truth***, ***Love*** and ***Anger***. Recently, a television documentary on the behavior of dogs provided a heart-warming metaphor for this amazing phenomenon. It showed that a dog is able to sense when its master is about to come home. At the precise time the owner made the decision to leave her office for home, the dog got up and went to the door to wait. It is the same when we are in the presence of truth, love and anger. We can "*sense*" them because they are sent out on the same frequency as our souls. Somehow, when we come into contact with these frequencies, we immediately recognize them. Sometimes we know they are coming before they are even sent toward us.

Take the Truth frequency for example. Youngsters Bryan, Julie and Maggie each deny breaking the flower vase. Mom looks over three apparently innocent faces and, in the voice only the guilty recognize, says, "Julie, do you have anything you want to say to me?" It is uncanny how often mom is right. To children, this is nothing short of a miracle, a mystery that will remain unexplained until they themselves become parents. We *know* when the truth has been spoken.

As sophisticated managers we sit in a conference room, witnessing colleagues distorting or camouflaging the truth, doing the safe political thing, saying what the boss "wants" to hear. Suddenly someone speaks the simple, naked truth. You can literally hear the breath of each coward being sucked back into their lungs. The truth demands just a moment of reverent silence as it fills us with fear and awe. The truth-speaker either is new and doesn't know any better, a veteran and doesn't give a damn anymore, or someone who has had a momentary lapse of sanity and has a sub-conscious wish to make an immediate career choice.

Among the senior executives at Union Central Life Insurance headquartered in Cincinnati, there are a couple of behavioral principles team members are not allowed to violate. We developed these while exploring how to become a high-performance team and I am amazed at how mantra-like they still sound. *"Team above Self, Truth above Safety."* For this incredible group, the good of the whole comes before the good of one. And if there is a choice between protecting yourself or speaking the truth, you speak the truth. Even if it means risking confrontation with one's boss, the truth always comes first. If the emperor has no clothes, he wouldn't take two steps at Union Central without someone pointing it out. For most of us though, the truth-frequency sends out such a shock-wave that we try to hide from it for fear it will cause us to come clean and change our participation. The Truth will indeed set us free, but not *for* free. Truth always carries a price tag. But, I must be quick to point out that truth brings wonderful rewards too, freedom being only the first installment.

Love is the same way. You *know* when you are in the presence of love because love brings you into connection with itself. When two people *love* each other, they don't analyze their relationship, adding up all the pluses of each other's character and subtracting all the minuses. Their lives beat in the same rhythm because love has brought them to a point of unity. However, since we live in a technological age, I feel bound to present the opposing view. Professor Cindy Hazan of Cornell University reports that couples "are biologically and mentally predisposed to be 'in love' for only eighteen to thirty months." She adds, "That is just long enough for a couple to meet, mate and produce a child." Love, Dr. Hazan concludes, is the result of a chemical cocktail made up of dopamine, phenylethylamine and oxytocin that simply wear off after a while. You could put that stuff in a spray bottle, for goodness sake. Maybe we should combine them into a vaccine so that love wouldn't wear off. While I am sure her office is papered with spreadsheets filled with reliable data, such findings leave me wondering if we are really talking about the same thing. If we are really talking about infatuation, then she is probably right, and indeed generous in her estimates. Thankfully, God's love seems to last longer and manifest itself in different ways.

Have you ever been on a work team that took on an almost impossible task, one that took each of you to the edge of who you were and then pushed you one step beyond? That project wove your respective strengths and weaknesses into a single fabric of unbelievable beauty. As .you all sat there exhausted, sharing a bottle of celebratory wine, 11:30 on a Sunday night, your 273 page report, still warm from the photocopier, finally put into the courier package for pick-up first thing in the morning, what did you feel as you looked around at your colleagues? As you remembered the animated arguments about direction in the early stages of the project, the times you were all so tired that giddiness took over and you could do nothing but laugh, the time the youngest and quietest member of the team suddenly showed wisdom and leadership far beyond her experience, prompting a major turning point in the whole process – was it *love* that you felt? Could it have been just another job that you had to do?

In an even grander way, God's love for all of his creation is visible all around us. By escaping from the angry participation of the manufactured world and basking in nature that invites you home again, how can you not see that God loves you? When Georgia and I drive up Happy Valley Road to our home it is exactly that way for us. We weave around a boulder mountain prickled with countless saguaro cacti, their arms always lifted toward their creator. We turn left on Whispering Wind and we know who is whispering and each day it's a new word. From our backyard we watch the sunset turn huge stones into gold and every time it's like the first time. In a sunset we, once more, have evidence of love. I see love too in a little Quarter Horse named "Hollywood." I experience it in his whinny as I walk up to his stall and in his eagerness to run the moment I settle into the saddle.

Perhaps you feel that it's a big leap from Happy Valley to the corporate boardroom. But just imagine a bottom-line, money-making, listed-on-the-stock-exchange business renowned for its truth and love. Think how little dis-stress there would be. No energy would be wasted on power plays and manipulations because truth eliminates such activity. Even difficult decisions would be unifying because they would be made in truth and love. Put these two together and you are well on your way to wisdom, a very desirable element for any organization bent on leadership in its marketplace. On the golf course, you'd tell your buddies what a loving corporation you work for while one of your employees would be telling her bridge club the same thing. While we are on a roll, think of a *government* characterized by truth and love. Now there's a stretch.

Why is it that we experience or witness truth and love so infrequently? What has distorted the natural resonance of the universe? Let's be clear that truth and love are as attractive to the human spirit as ever. Unfortunately, there's a problem with the receiver. In other words, there is nothing wrong with the tuning fork, but there is something wrong with our "ears." Guess what is messing up the music? You've got it. It's anger once again. We smash the bridge on the musician's violin and then wonder why we are not hearing beautiful music. We will not hear the peaceful melody of truth and love until we understand the role of anger in our lives.

I don't like the word **anger. Angerrr. Angerrrr.** The word can barely be spoken and I find myself bracing emotionally because the word is both evocative and provocative. In part I think it's because it resonates most uncomfortably with my entire Self. Because there is already an angry frequency within me, and perhaps within us all, it just feels like the anger "has my number" in some way. I create a vortex of despair because I get angry at the truth and when one denies the truth, there can only be more anger. I've even known myself to get angry at love and at the very people who love me. Have you ever hurt the ones you love? I have. Anger distorts the rhythm of my life and I want to change that, quickly and permanently.

Did you notice that when I started to write about anger, that I stopped talking about "you" and "us" and applied anger only to myself? That wasn't intentional until I discovered that that was what I was doing. Now it *is* intentional because dragging you into my anger won't help me deal with it. Nor can I be so dishonest as to write about it as though I don't have any but you do. One of the insipid characteristics of anger is that we seldom own it, preferring to assign responsibility for it to the object of our anger or even denying it altogether. It would be too easy to write about anger as though it was *your* problem, or simply *a* problem.

But I don't want to be safely remote. Anger is *my* issue and I bring it to all of my co-participations, including the writing of this book. This is not a weakness and I'm glad I know that that is what I do. Weakness is shown by *denying* the anger, not by admitting it. The frequency of anger is most acutely felt while we are at the Irritation Station, right across the road from the Institution Station. *Anger*, in the context of this discussion, *occurs when there is a conflict between the divine intention of our life and the behaviors and choices imposed on us by the institutions in our lives, or when we ourselves create a conflict through our own choices and behaviors.*

Anger can be a divine source of energy if we learn how to use it to move us to Insight and Integration. Again, you get to choose whether or not you want to join me in this exercise of spiritual growth. If you continue, my promise is that you'll read nothing that has not had a significant impact on my own journeying.

Anger does not discern, or even care, whether you are consciously aware of the conflict or not. Most of us, though, become almost super-sensitive to anger. We know we are irritated because we have not yet experienced a life of meaning. At work we know an angry E-mail when we read one. We can hear the Chairman's anger as he reviews the last quarter decline at the annual meeting in spite of his attempts to sound optimistic. As managers we sense the irritation or anger of our employees over the lack of balance between work and family or over some contrived policy change. Outside the office it is no different. You are no sooner seated in a restaurant and you can tell if it's an irritating place to work. Ever gone to an expensive restaurant – the kind with white tablecloths and wine with a cork – dropped $150 for two dinners, and had the distinct impression that you were annoying the staff by being there? In our marriages, without a word being spoken, we know that something is upsetting our spouse. As a professional speaker, I can tell you if I have an angry audience before anyone sits down. It is especially easy to do so on weekends. When I sense this, I'll often ask how many felt they had no choice but to attend the session even though it was on their personal time. When they are given the chance to admit that, once again, they were given no choice by the Institution, and that they are angry about it, we can clear the air and get on with something meaningful.

If we know anything, we know anger. And thank goodness we do because anger is an essential ingredient in our growth and the significant impact we can make on our world. My intention is to encourage the use of anger to gain insight about our life's direction. Remember: there are many situations in which anger is the absolutely right response. I get nervous when people claim to be content and calm about everything in their lives. Of course, I get even more nervous about those who use their anger to hurt others, refusing to gain insight into their Selves. **Anger is the soul calling to the Self.** When the Self does not answer, the tragedy of meaninglessness is the result.

So where does it all come from? The following framework comes from a long-time co-participator of mine, Glenn Taylor. Glenn was my first psychology professor so many years ago that he made me promise not to mention when. How he participated in my life during Psych 101 has influenced my entire career. If I have touched anyone in the thousands of audiences I have addressed during the last thirty years, Glenn gets part of the credit. He wouldn't want it, but he gets it anyway. Glenn read my book *Going Deep*, and that prompted him to initiate our reunion. In getting caught up on our respective journeys, Glenn shared his insights on anger. He and a colleague, Rod Wilson, have written about this in an excellent pastoral counseling manual titled, *Helping Angry People*. With their blessing I have combined their insights with my own and now offer them for your reflection.

Glenn and Rod propose that there are four major sources for our anger: *a breach of **Goals**, a breach of **Values**, a breach of **Expectations**, and a breach of **Self-worth***. Out of these four "breaches" two are about Self (Goals and Values), one is about others (Expectations) and one focuses on the interaction between Self and others (Self-worth). Throughout our lives we experience these breaches or violations, usually in various combinations, in many of our Institutional encounters. These encounters do not bring anger to us; rather, we bring anger to them. It's important to dig deeper and see what we can find for a fundamental reason. We cannot give up the responsibility for our own participation if we want to have a life of meaning.

1) A BREACH OF GOALS

There are endless books and speeches about the importance of setting and realizing personal and corporate goals. There are great and clever slogans like, "*If you aim at nothing, you'll hit it.*" and, "*If you can believe it, you can achieve it.*" Or how about, "*You can believe you can, or you can believe you can't – either way you'll be right."* And have you heard *any* speech about goal setting without hearing the story of how President John Kennedy challenged NASA to put a man on the moon by the end of the 1960s? On a slightly lower altitude, every New Years we *re-solve* some problem by setting yet another goal. Chances are we'll *re-solve* it again the next year. In many businesses, managers are given "KRAs" – key result activities – describing the primary goals they are expected to achieve. Sometimes their salary is based on the results. There are sales trainers who will tell you that success requires you to make ten phone calls before breakfast and at least five cold calls every day. Some of us, who are equally driven, post our goals on bathroom mirrors and refrigerator doors, often with pictures that represent that particular desire. Above all, we are told through many corporate training sessions, not to forget to make sure our goals are desirable, attainable, measurable – and whatever the other attributes of good goals are. The "measurable" part is stressed because, if we can't measure our goal, we can't manage our goal. This is all grand stuff. I believe most of it, I just don't do it. How about you?

Maybe one way to avoid being angry because your goals were breached is not to have any. But that's an impossibility for a couple of reasons. First, we act toward goals all the time, whether or not we are aware of doing so. Driving over to the supermarket for a pint of cream is a goal. Getting to an eight o'clock meeting on time is another. Applying your nail polish smoothly or shaving without cutting yourself are goals, too. These are not particularly grand and are not likely to make it to your bathroom mirror list, but they are goals nevertheless. Our routine lives are filled with them.

Of course, some of our goals, for whatever reason, gain enough momentum and importance that they rise above the mundane. They become a conscious and deliberate expression of our choices and behavior. We document them and labor toward their fulfillment. Lose forty pounds. Make our first million by the age of thirty-five. Marry for love and have two children. Keep a winter home in the Caymans. Learn Spanish. Stay with a job for at least two years. Double the production volume of our department. And on and on. Some of us are focused in our intentions and others of us just do the best we can as circumstances arise.

The second reason it is impossible to be goal-less takes us back to Chapter One where I discussed the "desires of our heart," those divine "assignments," the innate, contractual "intentions" that give meaning to our existence. The goal of helping in specific and unique ways to finish creation comes as standard equipment in *every* human being. There is no option here. So you can sit mindlessly on the curb your entire life if you want to, but the divinely-installed intention of your life is as real and potent as that of a great painter whose works hang in the Louvre, or a scientist who discovers a light source that cures AIDS. Just because a person is not becoming who they are meant to become does not mean that the goal to do so is any less present. God has created all of us, including your lazy, no-count brother-in-law, to be goal-*full*.

Let's reconnect to the anger issue. When your goal of buying cream at the supermarket and being back in fifteen minutes is breached because they've run out, causing you to drive another three miles to the Circle K and consequently missing the start of the Super Bowl, you start to get a little irritated. To make up for this added time you become a road warrior, cutting off two other cars and almost running a red light. Your wife was at the supermarket yesterday, you fume, why the hell couldn't she have picked up the cream then? Can't anybody around here do her job properly?

How about this one? It's ten after eight in the morning and you are sitting on a long parking lot usually known as the I-17. For all the money you pay out in taxes, someone should be able to design a highway that could handle the volume, wouldn't you think? What on earth is going on up there? Some idiot probably ran into somebody. And why your secretary set up an eight o'clock meeting you'll never know. She knows you're not a morning person. Through no fault of your own, here you go having your goal breached again.

And what about this scenario? You sacrificed everything – your social life, your health, and almost your family – to accumulate the kind of net worth that would allow you to retire young. The plan was that you and the family would then live in the south of France without financial worries. But then it turns out that, not only did you not make your target, you're flat broke. Apparently, you couldn't have had worse tax advice. All that money you were told was tax exempt wasn't. You're almost too stunned to be angry. Give it a few hours and then watch out! I can smell the lawsuit from here. For you, this is the mother of all breaches.

Anger in these vignettes is understandable and normal. If you were the central actor in each story and had both your minor and major goals breached in these ways, of course you'd be angry. (You may have gone over the line with the Super Bowl thing, but I'll get to that in a moment.) But here is the shocker about anger. Look at all the co-participators you've dragged into your anger: the dairy manager at the supermarket, your wife, the engineers who design highways, the IRS, your secretary, your accountant and a whole bunch of innocent bystanders who had the misfortune to be near you.

Now what about the curb sitter? While we know it is not true spiritually, he appears to have no goals at all. Is anger still there? I propose that, yes, it sure is. It's similar to not letting a greyhound run. Whether the dog gets the chance or not, its built-in intention is to run. Any time we spend *not* fulfilling the divine intention of our lives a restless irritation begins to set in because the "grand why?" is being breached. Remember this – *everyone* has a divine meaning and intention!

What is so deceiving about this experience of anger is that we seldom recognize it for what it is. In the other examples, the enemy is perfectly clear. One knows who to get angry at and what they should do to fix it. The curb sitter's inaction is an expression of anger at life itself, which is a rather amorphous target. He literally ends up fighting against his Self. Given that most of us, to some degree, are struggling to find and act on the grand why of our lives, we constantly have this irritation of breached divine intention as an undercurrent. This is why, when minor irritations happen to us, we get angry way out of proportion to the event itself, like the overreaction in trying to buy cream before the Super Bowl kick-off. Our anger always has a running start so little things can send it into overdrive.

This issue becomes even more complicated when we look specifically at the workplace, one of the most powerful institutions of our lives. Employers must deal with their restless employees who always gripe about something or other. Grievance after grievance is brought forward by the union stewards. "They ought to be grateful they have a job!

If they don't like it here, let them get a job somewhere else," are the irritated responses uttered in the boardroom. The sixteen "Breakfast with the President" sessions held in an attempt to ensure that every employee is clear about the goals of the company turn out to be one bitch session after another.

What might be going on here? It may be that the company is just a lousy one to work for with management enforcing compliance from the employees rather than giving them choices that could lead to real commitment. That scenario would lead us to an organizational and management intervention of some sort. *But,* let's say the company has bent over backwards to be good to its employees, paying them 15% above the national average, providing free tuition at the local college, sponsoring day care and so on. What are the underlying dynamics in this case? We have to go back to the idea of the irritating undercurrent. **Purposeless and passionless people cannot build a purposeful and passionate organization no matter how well they are treated.** This is why employees often appear ungrateful. They *are* grateful but there is a huge void in their life that is not being filled. They have not found the secrets to a life of meaning. Ultimately, until a person finds the "why?" to life, he or she will never truly buy into the "why?" of the organization. This begs the question: "Is an employer responsible for helping employees find the meaning of their lives?" Now if that question doesn't make an executive throw her or his hands up in despair, what would? However, if you are one, don't do that yet. We still have lots of thinking to do.

2) A BREACH OF VALUES

Contrary to popular belief, corporate values were not invented by Johnson and Johnson when someone contaminated Tylenol packages back in 1982. From the corporate perspective, however, that event launched organizations worldwide into reflecting on what decisions they would make in a similar catastrophe. Ergo, corporate value statements, philosophies, principles, beliefs and ethics were spawned. You get to pick your word. For me it is simply a matter of *making a conscious choice about what **we** as individuals, sincerely and honestly, in our heart of hearts, believe to be right, true and good.* It is what we *value* for the sake of the universal community, our co-participators. It is what an *ideal* world would look like, what an *ideal* relationship would be like, how an *ideal* boss would behave toward us, what we would experience in an *ideal* home or in an *ideal* relationship with God. Anything short of that ideal is a breach. Some breaches are so incidental you don't even know they've happened. Some are so devastating you aren't sure if you'll live through them.

The context in which you are trying to operationally apply your values is usually what influences your choice of what to call them. If you have a structured, systematic, scientific or intellectual perspective you are likely to discuss "ethics." Hospitals, for example, are much more likely to have an "Ethics Committee" than they are a "Philosophy Committee." Whether to perform heroics on an elderly patient who has just had a cardiac arrest isn't a philosophical issue alone. There are very objective medical and even legal matters to weigh into the decision.

On the other hand, when I was studying education we had to develop a "philosophy" of education. We didn't talk about "ethics" by that name so much. If you were discussing capital punishment with your neighbor over the backyard fence, you'd probably talk about "values." The context of religion often favors discussion on "beliefs." Who would say, "What is your philosophy about God?" I'd want to know what you "believe" about God. That just seems like a more *natural* way to put it. It doesn't really matter except to those who value debate. Spending hours "defining our terms" is an old corporate ploy designed to delay coming to a point while all the while sounding incredibly intellectual. Let us not fall into this deception.

Just as there can be a continuum of goals from the mundane to the majestic, so there is a continuum of values. For example, we all have values that, in the grand scheme of things, are not all that significant. Recently, Georgia and I went out to a Chinese restaurant for dinner. At a table across the aisle sat a guy wearing a "muscle shirt" (which in this case was a contradiction in terms), with arm holes big enough for his legs, and a filthy baseball cap on his head. Now my kids would say, "What's wrong with that?" I, being filled with righteous indignation, find that costume slovenly inappropriate for any place except a steel mill and then only on casual day. He breached my values, not that he cared. But the truth is, neither his nor my "value" about restaurant dress codes is likely to determine which of us gets to spend the rest of eternity in heaven.

Then there is the major league of values – the Ten Commandments. These are the values of such obvious worth and acceptability that one might conclude that they are universally accepted. *Most* people would at least claim such values as their own without too much debate. Mind you, there are lots of exceptions. The late Cambodian dictator Pol Pot, with a smile on his face, ordered the murder of two million Cambodians. Did Pol Pot have "values?" Our inclination is to say "NO!" but that is because his values were so far to the dark side normal people couldn't see them with a flood light. We aren't even close

67

to being *that* dark, but folks, we *all* have a dark side. There is a universal explanation which has to do with *The* ultimate value, the one without which all other value formations leave us untethered and dangerous. This ultimate value, this "Value of all values" is **Love.**

Between muscle shirts and murder is a huge range of values, like having a dollar store on Rodeo Drive. Somehow I bring to my co-participation a whole mess of things that I think are important or ideal to the life I want to live. At least right now I think they are. They range from table manners to my beliefs about God. These are my values, however well I am able to label them for you. You bring your own set of values to the table, too. Some of ours will match up just fine for the moment while others we'll never agree on. But like famed comedian Groucho Marx declared, "These are my principles, and if you don't like them, I have others." Unless we have the conviction of Joan D'Arc, some of our values are for sale and almost all of them are for rent.

Years ago I designed and facilitated a values conference for a group of Christian businessmen. They were given a sheet listing about twenty values, including one called "Salvation." The assignment was to rank the order of the ten values they considered the most important to their personal lives *and* their business. As you would expect, "salvation" was at the top of the list with everyone. Next they were given an envelope in which they found a dozen or so randomly sorted cards, each noting a certain value. There were "honesty" cards, "integrity" cards, and so on. By chance some matched their top ten values and some didn't. They also found a million dollars in play money. The "game" was to barter, buy, sell, trade or whatever they could do to end up with their top ten values *and* as much money as possible.

Whoever obtained the most ranked values and the most money won. Oh, did I mention that the key factor in all of this was that, for a group of thirty devout Christian men, there were only twenty "salvation" cards available?

I've got to tell you, this was fun to watch. Not for a moment did I doubt the sincerity of their Christian faith, but I also had no doubt about their competitiveness – they all wanted to win. Values were bought and sold like you wouldn't believe. I called the game off when the price of "Salvation" hit seven million dollars. The point, of course, was to illustrate that our "values" are very strange and slippery things. Regardless of our protestations to the contrary, when we get fully into the game of life, our values are constantly changing in shape, color and texture. We know in our personal and business lives that values should be forming the solid foundation for what we are all about. But much of the time it's like building a house on cement that won't dry. Sooner or later something is going to shift or tilt. We are all very human and I learned a long time ago not to condemn others for their struggle over values. We all struggle. Not one of us can "cast the first stone" of judgment and condemnation.

It would be great to think that there must be some grand universal value that all humanity espouses, one value that unites us all. As someone once said "It'd be a nice dream if we all dreamt it!" It's not the value of freedom or the sacredness of life that's for sure. We don't all agree on values regarding health or prosperity. We don't all care about the environment or the value of education. Values like equality, fair play, and honesty don't even come close to unifying us. Can anything bring us together and, if so, where do we go to find it?

A while ago Georgia and I bought a wall sculpture from Arizona poet and artist John Evans. The poem inscribed on it reads: *"Listen with your soul instead of your mind. Your soul hears with eternal wisdom, your mind is a product of conditioning and time."* This is good counsel. We've got to go to our souls for the answer, not to an ethics class or to some theological debate. We want to hear eternal wisdom out of our very soul and the language of the soul is love!

We are born with love infused throughout all our being. It's like our pores are lined with love. We want to breathe out love to others and we want to inhale love from others. Love is not a second-hand emotion, it is a primary one. This is *the* one universal value. In no culture on this planet do babies need to be taught to love their mothers. They all love their mothers and will do so until, and unless, that love is destroyed by anger.

The evidences of love are awesome and far-reaching, in both our personal and our work lives. As noted earlier, we know love when we feel it. Love gives meaning to our words. Without it we are just bags of wind. When is the last time you heard a corporate executive speak with love in his voice? How about a political leader? I watched a number of television evangelists interviewed about their views of President Clinton's indiscretions and, to be really honest with you, I had a hard time picking up any sign of love in what some of them were saying. Oh, they used the word "love" many times ("Hate the sin, love the sinner"). I just didn't feel love – but I did hear a lot of judgment and self-righteousness.

You can have a reputation as a master of change, as a corporate turn-around artist, but if there is no love in your intervention, the impact of your work will be temporary at best. Professional speakers can master the stage, bring tears to the eyes and the audience to its feet, but if they do not speak with love they might as well have stayed home. You can sacrifice your own ambitions and health for the sake of your family or even your employer if you want to, but if there is no love behind the sacrifice, you've just thrown your life away.

Love is also patient and kind. Not territorial, love is not interested in building empires and turfs. A manager whose life is based on love rejoices in the victory of another department as though it were her own. She doesn't respond in jealousy. A life founded on love does not "keep score" when others do hurtful things. We've all heard an angry person rant on about their intent to "even the score." Even if they are successful in doing so, a tie score does not win the game. A loving person is saddened when misfortune happens to others, even if that person is a competitor. A person whose values are based on love is protective of the communities and teams to which he belongs. Loving people tend to trust others rather than be legalistic and guarded in their relationships. They are hope-full people.

Many readers will recognize that the description of love in the last few paragraphs comes from the writings of St. Paul found in the New Testament, though liberties have been taken. Love brings us to our-Selves. Love brings co-participators together. Love is the energy source through which we can finish creation. It is the energy we need for successful families, businesses, religious faiths and schools. When God finished his part of creation, he said it was "good" because he saw love in every molecule. Without love we are dangerous "goods." Without love it does not matter what values we claim to have.

Here's a suggestion for you. Read over your corporate values document and count how many times you see the word "love" or at least a synonym for it. Until we learn how to lay down a foundation of love in our businesses, all we'll get from being on the Corporate Values Task Force is free coffee and muffins.

I've tried to show that we are created with a divine intention or meaning. We are also created with the need to love and be loved, the one universal value. When our goals and values are breached, our very identity, our humanness, is breached. No wonder we get angry.

3) A BREACH OF EXPECTATIONS

This third breach is the one that focuses primarily on others. Because we are all involuntarily linked as co-participators, it is quite natural to have some interest in the nature and quality of this relationship. So naturally, I get to wonder about you and you get to wonder about me. Will you do your part properly? Can I count on you, particularly if I take a risk in some aspect of my life? Do you care about me or are you out to hurt me? We are constantly looking around to ascertain how and what the co-participators of our lives are doing and how that will make our lives easier or more difficult.

So why is this so complicated? To see fully how critical our expectations are, we've got to bring our goals and our values back into the picture. Don't forget, you and I have an in-born meaning, an intention that we are heading toward, whether we know what it is or not. Everything is driving us toward that something. Consciously or sub-consciously, we *expect* to fulfill a wonderful and unique purpose. On top of that we have certain *expectations* about the "rules" or values of what the journey toward that goal should be like. Unfortunately, trouble is inevitable. All our co-participators have different goal expectations and different value expectations. If I were alone on this planet the road to success would be without hindrance of any kind from anyone else. Of course, it's also true that any "accomplishment" in such an isolated context would be absolutely pointless. Like it or not, we've got to accomplish our life's purpose in partnership with each other. On the other hand, if it was just the two of us, we could probably work something out so we didn't become a hindrance to each other. We'd just draw a line down the middle and each stay on our own side. However, there's a whole pile of people we have to deal with. I'm not sure what their goals or intentions are, and I'm really not sure what values influence their choices and behaviors. All I know is that there are certain things I want to accomplish with my life (meaning) and there are certain ways in which I want to accomplish them (values).

Expectations come spread over a very wide continuum. On the mundane end, I *expect* my desk chair to hold me up and to tilt when I lean back. I'd be angry if I fell over and hurt myself. On the majestic end, I *expect* God to answer my prayers. There have been times in my life when I've wondered where God was, but eventually, and somehow, I've always felt his guiding hand. I *expect* Georgia to love me for the rest of her life. This does not mean I take Georgia for granted but rather this expectation makes me want to be worthy of her love. So, given that I have a certain view of how the world should turn out, a breach of my expectations occurs *when any of my co-participators or co-participating factors, (humans, animals, weather, manufactured products, organizations, circumstances, etc.) hinder or prevent that view from becoming reality.*

73

A veteran race-car driver was once asked about the high number of rookies who would be racing against him. His biggest concern was that, with rookies, he just didn't know what to expect. With his own experienced peers, when a certain thing happened on the track, he knew they would fulfill his expectations about what they would do. In contrast, the other day the driver of a car in front of me had to slam on his brakes and swerve because the woman in the car ahead of him decided to stop for the yellow light. He *expected* her to go through the light because *he* expected to go through it, too. He used some very expressive sign language, to say the least. The fact that she was totally right and reasonable in stopping on a yellow light did not negate his feeling breached. This is what makes dealing with expectations so volatile. What is right or wrong depends on one's value set. She expected him to drive at a safe distance behind her and understand that, for her, yellow means stop if you can. He expected her to know he was in a hurry and that he didn't want to wait for another green light.

While we are at the mundane end of the continuum let's discuss why so many little and inconsequential disappointments make us angry. Let's start with the foundation we've already laid down, that most of us have an undercurrent of irritation because we have not yet fully found or fulfilled the divine meaning of our life. We start off restless and irritated and usually don't know why. This creates a pressure to justify the irritation and so we start looking around for reasons to be irritated. Mostly we look for unfulfilled expectations. Our mate leaves toothpaste to dry in the sink after he brushes his teeth. It's so irritating. Why are you responsible for sink cleanliness? Old dried toothpaste doesn't quite do it, we need more reasons, bigger reasons. Why can't he put his own dirty clothes in the hamper? You were not expecting to replace his mother.

And talk about a guy totally lacking in romance. Before you got married he brought flowers, surprise presents, you went dancing and enjoyed Sunday picnics by the river. Where did that all go? Now his idea of romance is the two of you watching the Phoenix Suns on pay-per-view with beer and pretzels. It takes relatively little effort to easily collect a dozen great sources of irritation, those areas in which your partner has clearly failed to meet your expectations.

For argument sake, let's say you are lucky enough to be married to an angel and, frankly, there are not many things you can complain about. What are you going to do for anger now? Well, just raise your expectations until she begins to let you down! If she really loves you, she should be able to read your mind and anticipate your every whim, as well as turn water into wine. Surely you can find a breach somewhere. If you just can't, start whining about how "she's just little Miss Perfect!"

The same "let-down" scenario happens in the workplace. Most labor-management conflict is over expectations. Labor expects management to share some of the profits with them if it's been a good year. This does not necessarily mean they expect to share in any losses. Managers expect their employees to give eight hours work for eight hours pay. The last time I read anything on what they actually get on average, I think it was five hours work for eight hours pay. No wonder owners get angry at their employees. This makes products much more expensive than they need to be which, in turn, breaches our expectations as consumers.

I could go on and on about various expectations, but I know you are onto the point. We have expectations from our relationships, from God, various institutions, our pet dog, and even from this book. We expect. We expect. We expect.

The reason we feel so breached when expectations are not met is that we expect in one direction. If we spent as much time and energy working on fulfilling what our mate expects *from* us as we do on what we expect from him or her, our relationships would be much more loving. If employees were to start everyday asking themselves, "What does my employer expect *from* me today?" it would be a much different workplace. If you are an irritated employee, you've already thought, "Yeah, but what about *them*?" You are right. Every manager and leader should begin their day asking, "What does my team expect *from* me today?" And instead of muttering about how God is letting us down, maybe we should spend some time reflecting on what God might expect *from* us. Maybe if we begin to watch how we might be breaching the expectations of our key co-participators, instead of watching how they are breaching us, we just might fan a little spark of joy and meaning in our lives.

4) A BREACH OF SELF-WORTH

This breach is the combined result of the other three. A breach of Goals + A breach of Values + A breach of Expectations = A breach of Self-Worth.

When you breach my goals, that is, when you deliberately get in the way of my doing what I want to do, I have to assume that you are also disparaging my goals – and me. If you thought my goal worthy and admirable, you'd want to help me reach it. Even if you truly care about me and are simply trying to provide wise guidance, I may feel breached anyway. Here is a common example. A university student says, "I intend to get my BA in Sociology." When we reply, "You're kidding. What good will that be? What can you do with it?" we have breached his self-worth. If then we add, "Why don't you get into technology? You're pretty good on the computer," we think we are affirming his self-worth. Think again. Or what about a woman's goal to move into a senior executive position because she really feels that she has leadership potential? Four times now, she has been passed over in favor of men with less experience and, from some perspectives, less talent. I don't care how confident she is; at some point in her solitary and quiet moments she will wonder if she really is worthy of such a position. I guarantee it.

When you breach my values, you breach the most intimate part of who I am. You denigrate those perspectives on life that I most treasure, perspectives that have probably been born out of the struggles of my life. Denigrate them and you denigrate me. When you curse using the name of Jesus Christ, for example, you breach my values and it angers me. Have you ever heard anyone yell out "Buddha," "Mohammed," "Krishna," or "Baha'u'llah" when they hit their thumb with a hammer? If you are prone to swearing, why don't you go breach someone else? Or, much better, quit breaching other people's faith-values altogether. Likewise, when someone thoughtlessly smokes in the home of a non-smoker, they violate their host's values and in essence say, "To hell with you and your house. You are not worth honoring."

When you breach my expectations you are implying that I am not worthy of your attention and care. A wife says to her husband, "If you talk to your boss the way you talk to me, you'd be fired on the spot." The way she sees it, he cares much more about meeting the expectations of his boss than those of his wife. So where does that leave her? A father keeps promising his young son that they will go away for a special weekend, just the two of them, and has been promising that for over a year. I know you don't need an explanation from me as to what is happening to that young boy's self-worth. Breaks your heart just thinking about it doesn't it?

My guess is that you generally agree with the examples given in the last three paragraphs. These are the breaches of everyday life. We've done them all and we've felt them all. But how do we explain what is behind violent anger? What about people who beat their spouses and children, drivers in a constant state of road rage, children who shoot their teachers, men who rape, and wars that kill the body, mind and spirit? These co-participators are fellow human beings caught in the breach. Sometimes they never escape.

Major anger usually means major breaching in the four key areas. So often within the violently angry is a relentless vacuum of goals, values, expectations and self-worth. Not only have they not found their divine purpose, they have no goals for this afternoon. Unfortunately, when a person has no goals he makes the convoluted decision that no one else should reach a goal either. "I don't know where I'm going, so I won't let that car get by me." "I can't hold down a job so I'll steal the money you made at yours." The same happens with values. "Nobody ever cared about what is important to me, so I don't care what is important to you." "I'll show you. My values are just as good as your values." When it comes to expectations it is likely that most of the key people in their lives have let them down, time and time again. To them, it seems quite reasonable to let everybody else down. That's fair isn't it? The "clincher" comes with the matter of self-worth: "Does anyone find value in the 'Why?' of my life?"

There have been a high number of executions in the United States in the last few years. Most of us saw the articles in the papers or heard about them on the news. With the exception of those few who were very, very close to the situation, the majority of us can't name one of those who died. And for the most part, you know what? We don't care. And our not caring proves the point they made with their lives. There is a terrible logic to this. No one cared about their lives and they didn't care about their victims' lives. Consequently, no one cared about their deaths either. Please don't equate this comment with an opinion as to whether they should or should not have been executed. Unless something went awfully wrong in the conviction process, we know they committed terrible, angry, violent acts against people who were just trying to find the meaning of their lives. Somehow some of us have been able to handle the breaches of our lives while others have not been able to. Does that make us better than they are?

I remember an obituary that read: "Thompkins, Harold – June 16, after a short illness. *He was a dishwasher at El Cantino Restaurant.* (Italics mine) Sadly missed by his wife Ellsa and sons David and Bryan…" and it went on to mention several others who loved him. In reading that, some might immediately conclude that this man didn't do anything meaningful with his life. But who do we think we are that we can come to that kind of judgment? Who writing or reading this is in a position to say that Harold had not found his divine intention, the secrets of a life of meaning? It is not about dishwashing, it's about engagement. It's the *unction* not the *function*.

The breach of all breaches is a failure to discover the divine meaning of our life. That means a failure to:

- stand clearly on the values that have been made precious through your struggles.

- look more at how you can meet the needs of others than at how they can meet your needs.

- recognize that self-worth is not determined by the amount on a paycheck but by the fact that God has no one else to do what you are meant to do.

God has, in a very real sense, put all his eggs in one basket – and you're carrying it.

What Is the Meaning and Purpose of My Life?

You can find the answer to the most difficult question in the Universe.

ACTION THREE

Because you are going to be working on your own anger, irritations and/or restlessness, you will need to be especially gracious to yourself. This can be sensitive stuff. But do understand that you absolutely *need* irritations in your life or nothing would change. You are *supposed* to be restless! This is where the seven secrets to a life of meaning begin to come into focus. It just may be that what has angered or disturbed you is also calling you to itself. Let's see if that is true for you.

Remember an important thing before you begin. The danger in my using words like: "irritation," "restlessness," and especially "anger," is that they are often and understandably associated with pain, resentment and other negative connotations. I want to present the flip side.

If a young man has been actively bothered by the pollution of the environment ever since his grade seven class went on a field trip to the National Forest Reserve, then maybe he will be driven by a negative "irritation." He will literally be angry at those who leave their garbage lying around. The forest has called on him for help to keep it alive. Let's also look at a ten-year-old girl who goes to her first orchestra concert. She is mesmerized by the artistry and magic of the first violinist. Even after the concert is over she acts like she is in a trance. Boom. There it is – the passion and purpose of her life! Now she isn't *angry*, but she has been made *restless*. Her life has been truly and wonderfully *disturbed* by the experience. She wants to do nothing other than bring beauty to the world through music. The violin has called her to release more of its power to soothe souls and heal wounded hearts.

I mention this because some people's lives are driven toward *correction* (the young man who wants to fix pollution) and some are driven toward *creation* (the girl in the violin trance). Both are to be applauded. With which one are you most closely allied? Maybe it's a little of both. We are going to see.

Your Assignment

1) Look back over the stations of your life (your work on Action Two may be of help) and identify four or five experiences or factors that have *disturbed* you to such a degree that when you think about them, you still get a twinge. That twinge could be a longing you feel, a righteous indignation or just the memory of a dream long ago put into your emotional storage shed. Note them on the chart on page 84.

2) Decide if those things are matters of "correction" or "creation." I hope you find a little of both.

3) Ask yourself what has kept you from responding to these *calls* from the Universe to your spirit. What has moved you away from them? What has blinded your eyes and plugged your ears? It can likely be traced to one or more of the institutions of your life. On this one do not respond too quickly because you will tend toward the obvious explanations like, "I didn't have the training," or "There were no opportunities." Look behind these things and you will find something quite different. For example, if your explanation is, "I didn't have the self-confidence," I encourage you to look deeper at which institution managed to convince you of inadequacy. Was it the school Institution? Your family Institution? It may even have been your religious Institution. This reflection is important because it holds the clues as to what you need to do to get your life back to its divine intention. It is so often the case that one or more of your Institutions has "talked" you into setting aside the discovery of your destiny in favor of complying with its own need to control.

Just knowing what influences have held you back is surprisingly freeing. Mostly what the "knowing" does is allow you to make a conscious choice about how much influence you will allow a particular institution to have over your life. Again, I am not advocating some internal act of revolutionary proportions in which you wildly and indiscriminately overthrow or discard these life systems that, for better or worse, richer or poorer, have led you to where you are today. People do that, some virtually and some literally. Virtual revolutionaries turn on themselves, often withdrawing into relational remoteness. Literal revolutionaries do what people like Ted Kaczynski, the infamous Unabomber, did and turn on others. Neither one is an effective strategy for finding a life of meaning. Confidently and quietly, you simply need to take back the choices that are rightly yours.

4) Rank these irritations or disturbances according to their "weight" or impact on your life. In other words, did one or more of these disturbances "get to you" more than others? If so, give it a higher ranking than something else that may have been a passing event in your life.

Disturbing Experiences	Correction/ Creation	Blocking Institution(s)	Weight on Life
1			
2			
3			
4			

Here is what we find in reviewing Actions One to Three. Action One had us take an honest look at those who are playing the game of life with us and deciding who is really on our team, and who is best able to contribute to our discovery of our meaning. Action Two invited us to take a broad assessment of the Institutions of our lives in order to determine what personal truths and learnings we can glean from our experiences in them. And now, in Action Three, we narrow the field a little more and focus on the major disturbances that may indeed be the voice of the Universe calling to us.

Next we will discuss how best to respond to the Universal call, or at the very least, keep ourselves open to it. Meaning is not far off.

Chapter Four

CHANGING YOUR REALITY

I see four factors that have the potential to put us in movement – movement that will get us from "here" to "there."

"Here" refers to what most of us know as our normal lives. "Normal" for many of us means a pin-ball existence that often has us being flung around by forces we don't control, scoring points only every once-in-a-while, bouncing off of various obstacles someone put in our way, and sooner or later ending up out of play. Though none of us wants to live that way, the usual reality is that our lives are very busy, giving us little time to think and reflect on our own meaning. This is the consequence of being consumed by the demands of our institutions and our co-participators.

"There" is the kind of life we almost don't think is possible in this world, a life in which we have asked *and answered* our "Whys?" A life of meaning! This is the ultimate state of spiritual maturity, characterized by wonderful earthy wisdom that lets us know how to minimize the likelihood of having our goals, values, expectations and self-worth breached. Not only that; when they inevitably are breached, somehow we are given the grace to use these irritations to create something even more rare and precious.

The four factors have to do with our: 1) **current reality** (the tendency to get stuck in our present and past) 2) **richly**

imagined future (our need to know the divine intention and meaning of our life) **3)** need for **self-disruption** (realizing that life is about un-doing as well as doing) **4)** power of **choice** (the final bridge between where we are and where we want to be).

Insight into these areas prepares us for the advent of wisdom. Not only will these four factors free up our personal lives – they are exactly the factors that will prepare institutions for real movement toward wisdom as well.

Acting on these four factors open us up to incredible wisdom although they are not in themselves the source of wisdom. Wisdom requires one to rise above all the complexities and contradictions of the mundane. When you stand on a high enough ladder, seeing how to walk through the most complex cornfield maze is child's play. If you have ever had the joyous frustration of weaving your way through one of these mazes, you know exactly the value of elevated wisdom. There is an Old Testament story of God giving Hebrew patriarch Jacob a vision in which he saw a ladder to heaven from which he could get the perspective he needed in order to see the wisdom of God's plan for him. We all need this heavenly perspective at some point. Between you and me, in my life I'd be glad to have just a foot stool most of the time; I can barely imagine the luxury of a ladder. What makes life so difficult is that we are trying to deal with maze overlaid on maze overlaid on maze.

In this chapter, I'm going to concentrate on the "**current reality**." (The next three chapters will discuss each of the other factors.)

When is the last time you had only one thing going on in your life? Usually when someone cares enough to ask,

"What's wrong?" we reply, "Oh, it's a *number* of things." At some point we've all said to a friend, "I've got *so many* things going on in my life right now, I can't even think straight." "Thinking *straight*" is another way of saying that you clearly see the direction for your life and that you have your meaning in view. When you *can't* see "straight," you've lost sight of your meaning.

In my experience, it is not the actual *number* of things going on in our lives; rather, it's the *interaction* between the various mazes that gets to us. The right turn in one maze seems to be the wrong turn for another. For example, if you work over the holiday weekend to get a report done for your boss, it might help you move further through the maze of your career path. However, because that decision takes you away from your family, it causes you to become even more misdirected, regressed or lost in the maze of raising your kids and being a loving partner. What are we supposed to do when faced with these conflicting choices? Most of us can handle two or three situations at one time but it doesn't take much beyond that to give us the feeling that we are losing control. Wouldn't it be terrific if we just knew what would be *wise* in every situation? Heck, it would be terrific if we knew what would be wise in even a *few* situations.

For me, there is only one Being who is high enough to see and understand all the interactive mazes of my life. God, I believe, is the ultimate source of wisdom. He alone has the highest perspective on what is happening to you and me. What is wonderful about God is that he has generously given every one of us access to wisdom with the intention that we help each other find it and use it rather than running around breaching each other and getting angrier all the time.

So here we are. Somewhere in our souls, overgrown and hidden by the mangle of our fears, the logical deceptions of our intellect, the often confining boxes of our various institutions, and the self-interested (if well meant) expectations of those who surround us, is the divine meaning of our life here on earth. We are responsible for participating this desired reality into existence through our choices. If our divine meaning has become clear to us, our choices are deliberate and focused. If we do not yet have that fortunate level of insight, our choices will be more far-ranging and inconsistent, and will often reflect our inner restlessness. At the same time, there are co-participators who also have an equally divine, though different, meaning than ours and who are also making choices. Sometimes positive and sometimes negative, these choices are all interactive and inter-consequential. That is, one participator's choice will enhance or hinder the intended outcome of another participator's choice. The choices we make today influence every tomorrow. This is because not one of our choices is isolated from the influence of other choices being made around us any more than you can have your own air to breathe. We all breathe each other's air and we all influence each other's choices.

Some of these enhancements and hindrances are deliberately focused. A teacher who goes out of her way to help your son win a scholarship, or a sexist manager who assigns an employee to work three consecutive weekends because she won't respond to his unwanted advances, are two examples. One is deliberately positive and the other deliberately negative.

Others alter our journey inadvertently though not accidentally. The customers who filled up a restaurant causing you to go searching for another one did not know they were altering the course of your life, but they did. At the second restaurant you struck up a conversation with the couple next to you during which you casually mentioned that you were trying to hire a new office administrator. Their daughter, it turned out, was looking for just such a position. Amazingly enough, you ended up hiring her. As you look back at the three years since that happened, you realize she was literally a "God-send." Such interconnectedness is foundational to human existence. *All* of our connections are God-sends; we just don't recognize them as such most of the time.

Learning to move and steer yourself through this unfathomable maze of interconnections happens on two levels. On the first level the major challenge is to discover where your life is heading, that is, your divine intention, the desires of your heart. Once you know where your own goal posts are, your *meaning*, the journey to that end is blessed with remarkable peace and joy. Even if you encounter turbulence on the way, peace and joy prevail to such a degree that it is obviously well worth whatever it takes to be there. Unfortunately, failure to find this purpose leaves you in a perpetual state of the opposite to peace and joy, namely, restlessness and anger. I feel that most individuals and most organizations are in this latter situation. (We'll get into this more thoroughly in the next chapter.)

Second comes the challenge of knowing how to maneuver in, around and among your co-participators on your journey to your fulfilled meaning. Since some co-participators are friendly and have your good at heart, you'll want to link up with them. That synergy might be fleeting or it may become a central part of your existence. Marriage is a good example of this. Maybe the two of you met through some amazing coincidence of choices. You fell emotionally and spiritually in love and stayed there. You cannot imagine life without this partner, this forever love. *Or,* you met at a point where you just really needed someone in your life. You married though it was hard to tell if this decision was based on love, lust or loneliness and you divorced two years later. You may wish you had made a different choice as you think back, but that brief connection was and is an important part of your journey.

Over the course of my life I have made choices that really moved me toward my life's purpose. I also made many that proved to be distractions and diversions from that purpose. I don't know why but it always seemed like the ratio was about one to five between the two respectively. My tendency was to look back at the not-so-smart choices and then become swamped with, at best, embarrassment or, at worst, incredible guilt. I usually chose "incredible guilt" (I wasn't raised Baptist for nothing.) Guilt, left to itself, always demands life-long re-hashings of what it was we did. Consequently, I became trapped in my own past, beating up on myself in an incredibly self-abusive way. This was not in a way that anyone would notice, mind you. This was self-inflicted abuse of the spirit, an inside job. On the outside I managed to look confident, gregarious, and together. I eventually realized that, if I was going to insist on re-living the past like I was doing, I might as well kiss the future good-bye. Kissing the *past* good-bye seemed like a better idea.

Here is what I want to pass along. You and I *must* learn to admit that even our poor choices have helped to make us who we are. A poor choice occurs when we link with co-participators who, it turns out, do not have our best interests at heart, *or*, it is we who do not have *their* best interests at heart. None of us like to admit it, but the latter variation happens as often as the first. Either way, it usually hurts and the pain usually lingers. It is almost as if those choices are trying to exact a tribute from us, like a pound of flesh from our soul. The tribute is not that you declare you are *glad* you made such a poor choice. That would likely be a lie and it would not free you. Only the truth can. The tribute being asked for is something like this: *"Today I would not make the same decision I made yesterday. But for various reasons and purposes that convinced me at the time, I **did** make that decision and I cannot change that. I may have hurt people and in all likelihood also hurt myself. For that I am truly sorry and will ask forgiveness and make recompense where I can. I give grateful and difficult admission to the fact that, as a result of that choice and its consequences, however severe, I have been shaken into becoming a more aware, patient, caring, careful and gentle person than I was. For that I am grateful because, as these qualities develop, my future choices will be more wise."*

Now, if what you regret is having made the decision to shoot somebody, all this is going to sound a little foolish. Remember, the tribute is meant to bring resolution between your inner Self and your past – **not** to achieve reconciliation with the other co-participators involved. That is usually another matter. Making a statement like, "I am grateful that I am now a kinder, gentler person because I have learned from what I did to you," will likely get *you* shot. But frankly, if the sentiment is truly heartfelt, the *intention* of this idea is still sound.

The point here is that we are not good at letting go and moving on. We have, particularly in North American society, almost a fetish about our current reality. We love current reality so much that we tend to re-relive it. And that applies not just to our *current* realities, but to our *past* realities as well. Actually, what we do is make our past realities our current realities. We live in the past to such a degree that it becomes our present. Even if those realities of our history are painful, we insist on revisiting where we've been. It's just like when we bang our head and it hurts to touch it. So what do we do? We keep touching it! We do that emotionally, too.

I can really understand this *past-time* and, as I've said, am prone to it myself with my positive, as well as my painful past. I am particularly fond of recalling those special moments when my kids did this and that – like the time during a "T-ball" game when six-year-old Nathan decided to chase a butterfly, rather than the ball, in right field. I even recall the bad events, like the time Karen fell and cut her head on the fireplace hearth and I had to speed her to the emergency room for the first time. These are the stories of our lives and they are precious. Have you noticed that, as your parents get older, they tell the same old stories over and over? This is because there is not much future to talk about and, since their *past* appears much richer than their *future*, that is where they dwell. Be patient with them, you are probably doing the same thing already and no one has told you yet.

Memories are to be treasured, particularly the ones involving those times when the world seemed so right and loving. Those are the moments when our anger went into remission. That was when we truly felt the smile of God in a most unusual way. "Letting go" does not mean we shouldn't remember. It's like how you want it to be with your relatives. You want them to visit every once-in-a-while, but usually you don't want them to move in with you. Visit your memories, just don't move in with them.

Look at how the past pervades our business lives. The agenda for a typical business meeting starts with "*Old* business." Can you imagine saying to a fellow committee member, "Let's get to the meeting early, I don't want to miss the *old* business?" That would be like going to a restaurant for leftovers. Some groups open their meeting with "Business *arising* out of the minutes." That sounds like methane gas escaping from a swamp. If you lit a match the whole place would blow. Yet others, with a penchant for even more details, open with "The reading of the Minutes," which is the act of going over the documentation of yesterday line by line, minute by minute to ensure it is recorded right. These unimportant phrases betray our preference for clinging to yesterday as long as we can. No wonder corporate change takes so long.

The reason we prefer to manipulate and re-manipulate data from yesterday is precisely because it provides an escape from the God-given responsibility of creating tomorrow and fulfilling our divine meaning. That sounds harsh and will probably arouse some defensiveness from more than a few readers. But let's admit it. We feel confident and in control when we revisit what we did yesterday. The idea of moving into the future with a leap of faith frightens us into repetition, redundancy and restraint.

You need to understand what happened yesterday. Facts and data will help you do that. Learn what needs to be learned, then let it go. It's over. Please don't beat-up people with the past, unless you want them to repeat the past. Most importantly, don't beat yourself up with the past either.

Still, in one way or another we all have a way of clinging to our past and current realities. Have you ever helped a child stuck in a tree? You can't quite reach her so you encourage her to "just let go" knowing you are more than able to catch her. She will wonder if there is another option because letting go seems like a truly frightening choice.

She may be terrified by her current reality, but at least she has a grip on *something*! What if she lets go and ends up in an even worse state? It is easy for *you* to say you'll catch her, but the child sees only the danger of falling three or four times her height.

What are you hanging on to? What are you afraid to let go of? If you are at all like me, there are portions of your past and current realities that you cling to, playing them over and over like a favorite record. We get stuck in the "golden oldies" of our memories and when we do, the part of our *past* we cling to becomes part of our *present*.

Consequently, we come to a rather thin edge. Memories of experiences are a vital part of our lives. They allow us to tell stories of the past to our children and our children's children. They allow us to learn and grow in wisdom. Understand what you have been through, learn what you need to learn – and then move on. That applies to wonderful positive memories as well as hurtful negative ones.

We become locked in our current realities for one of three reasons. Some current realities perpetually hurt us, jolting us with the sharp shock of guilt for past choices made poorly, or with the pain of personal inadequacy. We hang on to them because we feel we deserve the abuse and punishment. Other current realities have made us very comfortable and safe. Why would we want to leave them? And finally, some current realities seem glued to our souls because we are meant to take action toward them, or because of them, and until we do they will continue to bother us.

Current Realities that hurt you are those experiences that still cause you pain as you think about them. You probably referred to at least some of them in your notes in

Action Two. We all have them even though we react differently to their memory. Some criminals are described as "showing no remorse" for hurtful choices they made. Others among us generate enormous guilt for experiences they had relatively little to do with. Of course there are other realities that just seem so unfair they can cause feelings of hopelessness. Hopefully you and I will find ourselves somewhere between these alternatives.

Current Realities that make you comfortable and safe seem at first glance to be very desirable. Shouldn't most of your life be built on such reality? Not necessarily. That would be like inhabiting so luxurious a room at a resort that you never venture out to play in the ocean waves or visit the local marketplace. For example, many young people delay independence precisely because things are so comfortable at home. Usually, this is not a good thing.

Current Realities that seem to have a mysterious grip on you are usually reflective of "unfinished business" in your life. This, over the years, becomes one of those "I'll always wish I had..." reflections. It may be that the Universe planted an idea in your mind and heart and you've not responded to it.

The problem many of us face with our current realities is that we don't know how to let them go and move on to new experiences. This causes us to literally perpetuate the past instead of creating a future. When this happens, our memories become our future. If we do not see any new experiences coming our way, the only way to deal with the vacuum is to relive old experiences. What else can one do? The critical lesson we each need is to ensure that our lives are filled with interests and variety, and never lose our sense of purpose and meaning.

Regrettably, many in the corporate world live and die on "data." "Manage by *facts*," is the philosophy of many corporate managers today. I understand the value of this strategy but it conceals a huge trap that prevents the emergence of leadership. "*Leading* by facts," is a contradiction in terms. You can only lead by *faith* in what is possible wrapped in a *vision* for a world yet to be. If you only "manage by facts," you are managing by yesterday's results because that is the only place you can find facts. All data, all facts, come from *yesterday*. There really is no data about tomorrow that you can truly count on. About fifteen years ago, at a conference of insurance people, I asked them if anyone had AIDS in their ten-year-plan. Who knew then what tragedy we were running into? And which person reading this book knows what epidemic or catastrophe we will face next?

It was just another Saturday morning in September for popular CNN reporter John Holliman. He went out to get some syrup for the weekend pancakes. John Holliman never came home. He was killed in a traffic accident, leaving his wonderful wife and his five-year-old son Jay to wonder, "Why?" CNN showed viewers the screen-saver on Holliman's computer. Scrolling across the screen were the words, "*Jay Holliman's dad is very proud of his son.*" If that doesn't make every dad reading this pause just for a moment, nothing else in this book will. Why don't we all change our screen-savers to messages of love, hope, faith and commitment? If you were to be suddenly taken from us, what would you like your family and teammates to find on your computer screen? Please – the next time you are in the office, create that message.

What I am trying to do is remind us all that life is an act of faith. With all the instant and universal information available at the click of a mouse, with all of our amazing insights and scientific advancements, we still have no conclusive idea about tomorrow.

Getting stuck in our past is an evidence of anger. It means we feel breached in some way, and we find ourselves determined to not leave the past until there is revenge or reconciliation. How very common, how very human, and how very defeating of the Self. Logically, never mind spiritually, resolution cannot happen in the past. It only happens in the future, when we get back into line with the divine and the richly imagined intention of our lives.

What Is the Meaning and Purpose of My Life?

You can find the answer to the most difficult question in the Universe.

ACTION FOUR

Your Assignment

The goal in this chapter's assignment is *not* to rid yourself of various memories but to loosen the grip you have on them (memories have no grip on you) so you can move to a new and better place.

Pick no more than *five* current realities in your life. Any more than that and you may start abusing yourself with discouragement, guilt will flare up and you might feel the inclination to jab sharp objects through your skin.

Now write a sentence or two describing each reality. I find that the more I try to explain a current reality, the more excuses and distortions seem to creep in so just jot down a headline, so you'll end up with five headline sentences. Here are several examples.

"When I was nine I was at a parent-teacher meeting with my father and he told the teacher that I was not very bright and she shouldn't expect very much. I've never forgotten that and I'm thirty-five years old."

"I lost three jobs in a row because of my drinking and ended up having to declare bankruptcy this past December."

"I had actually been awarded a drama scholarship to a University but I didn't go and I have always regretted it."

"My parents built a basement suite in their home for me and are charging me hardly any rent. This should work out until I get married."

"I keep thinking I've 'got a book in me' because of how unusual my life has been. But everyone keeps telling me that publishing a book is almost impossible these days. I'm almost seventy-one years old so maybe it's too late."

"I hear music. I mean everywhere – even in my sleep. I've written a few songs but have never really done anything with them."

"Last week my doctor confirmed that I have breast cancer. Right now I don't feel any sense of purpose to my life at all. What's the point of anything?"

Did you notice as you read these examples that you knew exactly and immediately what you would say to the person who wrote them? It is so easy to see the current realities in someone else's life and so easy to coach *them* to move on. That's why I'm going to ask you to put yourself in a few of these situations.

Pretend the one about the parent-teacher meeting is your headline and step back to look at it. First, what an awful thing for a father to say and no wonder such a hurtful memory would linger and create limits on what you do with your life. But look at this – is there any way in which this negative experience happened as a result of a choice you made? Of course not! You were hurt by a "co-participator" who chose to diminish you. You had a breach of self-worth as well as your expectations. All that because of someone else's choice. Now *you* have one to make. Some of your painful current realities came from the choices of others and you do not deserve them. You are reaping what you did not sow. What would you have said to the person who really wrote this headline? Say the same thing to yourself.

Let's try the one about drinking and bankruptcy. Obviously this one is totally different because it's about choices *you* made. Find and express the reason. Say or write, "I made this choice because…" Out loud is better. The reason may sound selfish and shallow but that's because you are in a different place now and that reason doesn't make any sense to you anymore. Some form of anger drove you to drink and to eventual bankruptcy. What caused you to be so angry? What *breaches* were going on in your life at the time? You've paid a high price and it is important that you learn something worth that kind of tuition. Declaring why you made those choices and what you learned as a result is the key to being able to move on.

Finally, we'll look at the one about the person who hears music in his head. Here, no one is doing anything to anyone. Of course in his head there may be a romantic song that will never be sung at a wedding, a chorus that no children's choir will ever sing at a pageant, or a hymn that will never move people closer to God. When you think about it, non-action actually gets pretty costly. Can you imagine being given a truly valuable gift and saying to the one being so generous, "Thanks, but I'll never use it." Unfortunately many of us do this to God all the time. We are given gifts of dance, music, art, intellect, language, compassion, healing and on and on and we never use them. Do you think you'd be given a gift of such value if there weren't also circumstances available that would bring that gift to life? Batteries *are* included! I learned a long time ago, that when God gives you something he intends for you to use it.

Have you noticed that current reality always leads to a choice? And that is the last part of this assignment. What choice do you have to make now? This assignment has tried to *encourage* you to understand what happened to you, either through your own choices or someone else's. Remember, *not* making a choice is *not* one of your choices. You *must* make a choice. Doing so will begin to move you to a richly imagined future in which the meaning of your life becomes completely obvious to you and those around you.

Chapter Five

YOUR RICHLY
IMAGINED FUTURE

I f one more motivational speaker tells me I must have a goal, it will be to stop listening to motivational speakers. I mean, let's move on here! Been there. Done that. Surely there is more to self-motivation (and *all* motivation is *self-*motivation) than just setting goals.

Maybe I feel this way because "goals" seem so selfish most of the time – how to make millions, how to get to the top, how to get everything you want. It feels so shallow, though maybe that's because I don't have millions. But you don't hear many speakers telling you to set a goal about being more loving or gentle or filled with joy, do you? It's always about *things.* When has anyone encouraged you to tape a picture of a homeless person on your refrigerator so that you will always be focused on eliminating homelessness? How about a picture of the local food bank, held in place by a magnetic watermelon? On the other hand, you *will* frequently be encouraged to tape a picture of a Ferrari, a Maui beach house, or a model half your weight on the fridge door or bathroom mirror. We're told the secret of success is to have a constant mental picture of everything we want. And indeed, those *things* are easy to imagine. In contrast, this chapter is not about *things in* our lives – it's about the *purpose of* our lives, our divine intentions. How do you tape *that* to anything? What can we use for an image?

A brilliant graphics designer and communicator named Robert Burns came up with the phrase *The Richly Imagined Future* and I fell in love with it. It's evocative, powerful, energetic and sexy. Roll each word around in your mouth and mind as you say it, as though you are tasting a fine wine. Put the emphasis on the word *richly*. Say it slowly like you are eating an incredible cheesecake, climax on the '*ch*' and then quietly exhale a satisfied '*lee*'. The phrase creates a lot more satisfaction than "goal" or "mission statement" don't you think?

The word *imagined* is just as wonderful. However, you need the eyes and heart of a child to really appreciate it. Have you ever seen a child's eyes the first time she looks down the main street of Disneyland? That's the *wonderment* of imagination we need here, too. Parents are more likely to look down that same street and imagine long line-ups and eternal waiting for everything. I was reminded recently that all children have this readiness to wonder no matter how poor and destitute they are. I was raised on the edge of the Sahara Desert where my parents were missionaries. This past Christmas I had their fifty-year-old 8mm missionary movies transferred to video for them. In one scene they were giving out T-shirts and shorts to the native kids in a leprosy village who had never seen, never mind owned, anything so wonderful. They had the look that says, "What do these *wonders mean?*"

The heart of life is coming to understand what the *wonders* of our existence mean. Unfortunately, too many of us go to our graves saying, "I wonder what the wonders *meant.*" That is the *saddest* of all unanswered questions. So think of *i-magi-nation* as *I-magic*, recalling the magic that lies within each of us and maybe we will come close, or at least as close as adults can, to experiencing the awesome power of this incredible and divine gift. The wonder of imagination! Everything that exists in our world began as imagination. And all that is possible is wrapped up in this gift which is why it is, at once, the most freeing and imprisoning force known to us – depending, of course, on how we use it. Our own unique personal world is *full* of wonders, each of which illuminates the path to our richly imagined future. See enough wonders and your way will be well lit. You will have no trouble finding the meaning of your life.

What picture do we richly imagine for our lives down the road, since that is where the future is? Can we make that picture so bright, so real, so vibrant, so digital, so filled with color, so holographic that it's almost like we could step right into the future's frame? Can we make a virtual reality for our souls?

Yes we surely can! But before we attempt to create a composite picture of our life's wonders, let's look briefly at the concept of "future." For most of us the immediate tendency is to think of the future as a time-defined phenomenon, which of course, is what it is. However, it is more than that. What happens in even the next hour is the culmination of what wonders you recognize and the choices you make in response to them.

Let's say you have yet another meeting with the Reengineering Committee in exactly fifteen minutes. Let's also say that you'd rather go in for a root canal. This meeting is the result of six months of politicking, backstabbing, and questionable, rather shady negotiating, almost to the point of high crimes and misdemeanors. Step back for a moment and just imagine what is about to take place before it actually unfolds. As you think about the meeting, also begin to imagine your future, at least the next hour or so of it. Imagine the meeting room and that certain people will sit in certain strategic places. Imagine the ineffective chairperson who, in the last meeting, totally lost control of the proceedings. Imagine a sharp and cutting tone to the discussion because they've all been like that. Without question your image is justified. It is not hard to see what future you are getting braced for, is it? For you the future is happening already on physical, emotional and spiritual levels. And it is not good for you.

You are *imagining* all right, but not *richly* imagining. You are imagining a poverty to your spirit and to that of your co-participators. To *richly* imagine is to anticipate a situation that leaves everyone better off than when they started, in essence *spiritually* more wealthy. In our committee meeting example, we might richly imagine a true desire to understand each other, a strengthened sense of teamwork, a greater appreciation for the differences between team members, a genuine caring for the welfare of people affected by any outcome and, of course, the sheer joy of a wise decision. After all, there are no greater *wonders* than the ability to truly understand another human being, to experience colleagues working unselfishly toward a common purpose, to value the amazing differences between people, and to care in the purest and deepest way for the welfare of others. And what could be more amazing than to actually be an instrument of wisdom?

I know a few of you reading this may be thinking; "Give me a break, it's only another damn committee meeting!" This is exactly the point. It is **not** just a meeting. It is one of the *wonders* of your life! Again, think about the mind-boggling complexities of the universe that culminated in those people ending up in that room at that time. When we can't see the wonders, we are doomed to meander through life without ever finding our intention. When we can't see the wonders we can't make the choices that will lead us to the spiritual wealth that most of us desire. So first we must learn to see the wonders and then learn to make positive and wise choices in response to those wonders. Indeed, when we truly see the wonders, it is almost impossible to make bad choices. This is how the *richly imagined future* becomes present in our lives now. *This* is how we live a life of meaning!

Very few people see *wonders* in their workplace. This is a strange and sad circumstance because we can see them elsewhere. Here's a scene for you. An executive who appeared so uncaring and tough at work actually managed to attend his daughter Melissa's grade four play, "*The Legend of Johnny Appleseed.*" Melissa was Mrs. Johnny Appleseed and she insisted that her dad and mom sit in the second row (the first one being "Reserved") right near the center aisle. They could see her white bonnet as she peered through the curtains to be sure they were still there and ready for the wonders they were about to see. And wonders there were! It went the way grade four plays are supposed to go, with kids forgetting their lines or saying them either too quietly or too loud, the teacher's constant prompts from backstage, the miscued curtains. Each one was a wonder. And then the wonder of all wonders – Melissa's only line rehearsed a thousand times at dinner, in the bathtub and the last thing before sleep: *"Oh my dear husband* (that part always made the other kids laugh and it did this time, too) *do not be discouraged, for people around the world will eat from the orchards you have planted."* I do not even want to meet the parent whose eyes are not filled with tears of wonder in such a situation.

There are wonders all around us, in every common circumstance. The more we recognize them, the richer we are. An immigrant coming to this country from an impoverished situation just can't get over the wonder of a grocery store. A lot of us find shopping to be a nuisance. We've thrown away more food than they've eaten. For the immigrant it's one of the most amazing adventures of his life. Aisle after endless aisle of food, so wondrous he is afraid to even touch anything. I remember speaking at an all-employee rally of good, hardworking, salt-of-the-earth folks from the shop floor who had never before attended a company sponsored event of any sort. That's kind of hard to believe, but it was true. Coffee, muffins and juice were lavishly laid out for the participants that morning. I got there an hour before the session started and found over a dozen people already there. They were standing in a line about six feet from this breakfast feast, not a word being said. Seeing me, one of them turned and asked in wonder, "Are we allowed to have that?" As I reassured them that it was all for them, I thought that if the session had been for an executive group weary of such events, they probably would have complained that it wasn't a hot breakfast. May we never lose the thrill of wonder.

Our everyday world is wonders-full! Your very life is wonders-full! Maybe if we could see all the wonders under our sky there would be fewer wars, less crime, fewer street kids, happier marriages and less burnout and anger in the workplace. By doing so we can learn the secrets of a *richly imagined future,* the fulfillment of our divine meaning. One of the most wonderful bits of terminology from technology is the word *refresh.* When we make changes to a configuration on our web site, we have to click on *"refresh"* to actually apply those changes. Richly imagining our future should refresh us in much the same way.

THE SEVEN SECRETS TO A LIFE OF MEANING

I don't know who decided there were only "Seven Wonders of the World," but I thought I'd follow suit and suggest that there are *seven secret wonders* to keep in mind as we imagine our future and the meaning of our lives. These are seven spiritual *qualities* – not *things*. Let me illustrate the distinction. If you are looking for a new painting to hang in the family room of your house, it is not likely that you could describe what you want in sufficient detail so that someone else could get it for you. Only *you* will know the true "it" when you see it. Buying a painting as a *thing* is easy. On any weekend in strip malls around the country, you'll find cultural entrepreneurs selling paintings out of the back of their trucks or in little white tents. Most of these works, however, will not fit with your intention. They will be only *things* to you because you do not connect with them on any meaningful level. Eventually you will find "the one," your own particular "it." It's like having a spiritual reunion. This painting was "yours" since it was created in another place and another time and now you have found each other. This *thing* matches exactly the *imagining* of your mind. As you admire it on your wall you think, "It *goes perfectly* in this room!" These thoughts are intended to help you *go perfectly* with your future as the painting goes perfectly with the room.

The meaning of your life will be known through these seven secrets – these seven wonders of the meaning-filled life.

1) The Wonder of Love and Family

Writing only a few paragraphs to explain this first secret is an almost impossible task. Poetry or music would probably be a better medium than prose. Who, having known love, has not wondered at its magic? And is there a sadder, more powerless state than to feel *unloved*? Assuming you would rather feel strong than powerless, love has to be part of your richly imagined future. Literally look for love! Make love an essential ingredient or quality in any option you choose for your future.

The most obvious application of this secret is to your relationships. Certainly love must be the basis of your most intimate connections. Spiritual connection cannot be maintained without it. Can there be anyone reading this who is not looking for his or her "soul mate," or who has not found such a treasure already? Such intimate love is an impenetrable weave of what the Greeks call *eros* (a sexual love) and *agape* (a transcendent love, the Love of loves, God's love). Not all of your relationships will have this depth of foundation, but love can play a part nevertheless. Approach *all* of your co-participators with *philia* love – a brotherly love. Your boss, the paperboy, the UPS woman, your committee members, even the telemarketers who phone in the middle of your dinner – all are deserving and needful of your love. When you exude love in this way, you will receive it back a thousand times over. Loving others gives meaning to their lives, and in return they will give meaning to yours. You will not find meaning until you have shown love to those around you.

I do not mean to limit this to one-to-one human love, as wonderful and essential as that is. Situations and contexts can exude love, too. Pick those that do and your future will be much happier. For example, Georgia and I are so grateful about where we decided to build our new home, because our street is a *loving* street. We all know each other and not just by name. We *meaningfully* know each other.

We eat regularly in each other's homes, watch out for each other and do all the other things that loving neighbors do. There is another not so loving side to our situation, however. Our street is part of a much larger community and once a month we get a community newsletter. Eighty percent of it features people complaining about things like barking dogs, ugly "yard art," weeds on the neighbor's property and on and on. Every time it comes out we increase our gratitude that we don't live on the streets where there seems to be so much bickering. So, if you are choosing a place to live for at least part of your future, short-list only loving places – and *then* pick the one with the best view.

I link "family" with love for a reason. Deep family love – "*storge*," the Greeks call it – is a universal life context that I wish for everyone. Many of us have made a commitment to family, the most treasured of all relational options. Once you have this amazing occurrence in your life, your choices about your future must factor in the family. Since the meaning of life and the meaning of family are inextricably connected, your richly imagined future and that of your family are also interwoven. To make choices that are good for one and not the other is not very wise. Even if your richly imagined future has to go through the sad prospect of a divorce, I encourage you to hold love for family paramount as much as you can.

For some, of course, raising a family in the traditional sense is not part of their richly imagined future. *The Last Temptation of Christ* was a provocative movie that was not well received in religious circles. The devil, you may recall from the authorized story, tempted Christ with promises of power and riches, all to no avail. The movie takes over at that point and has Christ imagining what it would be like to have a loving partner, the incredible joy of his own children – the indescribable wonder of family. This was the test of all tests, the movie suggested, the one and only temptation that almost caused Christ to abandon his meaning, his divine intention of bringing salvation to a broken and angry world.

Many devout people go through this very struggle. Sister Beatrice was the Executive Director of a major hospital I consulted with years ago. A more real, loving and spiritual woman I have not met. Over dinner we were having one of our many personal conversations and she shared with me her struggle about family. Having passed the fifty-fifth year of her life, she said, she was still coming to grips with the fact that she would never be a mother. This had been a major torment for her and, frankly, I was surprised by the anguish in her voice. I thought, insensitively, that religious men and women had worked that stuff through before signing up. But it was her greatest "temptation," too. It is no accident that Roman Catholics use family designations like Sister, Brother, Mother, and Father in their organizations. So even if your divine intention calls for life-long celibacy, love of family will be in there somehow. Know that and use it. Choices that reflect love and focus on family, however you may define it, are much more likely to take you to a richly imagined life of meaning.

The same thinking applies to how you choose the work on which your life will be spent. Some places are *loving* places to work and some are sheer hell. Believe me, I could show you absolutely miserable and angry work environments that are devoid of love. But you probably don't need me to find them for you. If the workplace doesn't feel loving, don't work there unless it's the only choice you've got right now. And if that's the case, maybe you are meant to work there in order to help it *become* loving. May God give you strength!

As you search for your meaning, keep your spiritual antennae tuned to love. Love calls you to itself. You will hear that call better if you ask your Self a few questions. Does this place feel loving and can I bring love to it? Is this situation likely to treat me in a loving way and will I help it do so by being loving myself? Will those people genuinely care about me and will I care about them? If the answer is yes, you may have found at least part of your divine intention. You'll know it if you have because it *goes perfectly* with your life.

2) The Wonder of Giftedness and Creativity

Each of us has been brought into this world to help bring all that is meant to be into existence. This is the grand intention for all human participation. God's *imagination* and his *intention* are the same thing. We *are to literally act out God's imagination through our lives.* (I've got to tell you, that thought gives me the shivers!) This is one powerful secret!

When you patiently take your eighty-year-old mother grocery shopping, you are acting out God's imagination. When you take your kids fishing on the weekend, you are acting out God's imagination. When your children play under the hose on a hot summer's day, they are acting out God's imagination. When you have the difficult task of laying off an employee, try to act out God's imagination. When you develop your departmental strategic plan, remember that you are acting out God's imagination. So too with how you drive, how you play golf, how you treat the bellman at the hotel, how you pass a homeless person on the street, and on and on we could go. I am acting out God's imagination with every speech I deliver and every word I write. Can you think of anything more awesome? Can you think of a higher standard against which to measure the meaning of your life? I can't.

But what does this incredible secret mean? It means the meaning of your life will be in pattern with God's imagination. If you find yourself involved in something about which you are uncertain, say to yourself, "I am acting out God's imagination." If that statement feels incongruous with what you are doing, I guarantee that you are moving away from a life of meaning. Nothing will bring you greater joy and meaning than to be an instrument of God's imagination.

Not only that, we have brought with us a pallet of gifts and strengths with which we color that part of creation set aside specifically for us. This circumstance should send us into unbridled ecstasy. However, here is a sad reality. Most people are underutilized. In other words they have gifts and strengths that are not only not exercised in their various activities, such as work – they aren't even recognized.

One of the things I do to relax and create is paint old hand-carved wooden bowls. The result is best described as a form of primitive southwest folk art, which is another way of saying that I don't paint particularly well. One evening while I was painting, Georgia asked me how come I didn't use a particular color since I had used all the others repeatedly. The fact was I didn't even know I had that color available to me or I would have painted the bowl much differently. Many lives are exactly like that, particularly mine.

I am writing this at the age of fifty-four. Some of my thoughts lately have focused on trying to understand why

I have not used all my "colors" more effectively, aggressively, courageously, efficiently and thoroughly over my years. A couple of things drive these thoughts. One is that many friends are talking retirement, which I refuse to even entertain as a serious topic. For me, and I hope this attitude changes soon, the idea of retirement creates an image that I am in the last inning of the game. If I am going to "win" by accomplishing all I am meant to do with my life, I'd better start getting some runs now. I feel pressure and regret about not having played as well as I could have earlier in the game.

The second factor comes from watching my children make their life choices. On one hand I find myself thinking, "They are young, they have lots of time." On the other hand I desperately want them to get on with the intention of their lives because I wish I had not wasted so much of *my* precious time. You can guess which viewpoint they are most receptive to. After high school Nathan found himself a job instead of going immediately on to college. Guess how many times I've mentioned to him that he needs more education and that he should get it now? Karen took two months off this summer to travel around Europe. Guess how many times I've mentioned that she could have finished her degree instead? Erin is patiently waiting for her new massage therapy practice to build up through word-of-mouth. Guess how many times I've pointed out that she needs to launch an aggressive marketing campaign? Ryan does some crazy things with what little money he has. Guess how many times I've mentioned what he should really pay off his debts before buying something else? Were I as wise as Harry S. Truman who once commented, "I have found the best way to give advice to my children is to find out what they want and then advise them to do it." While reading *A World Waiting to be Born*, I felt relief from M. Scott Peck's statement, "It is crucial to note that children usually have a far better sense of their own vocation than do their parents." Thank God for that. All of this, I know, is nothing more than my wishing I had made better choices when I was their age and that I had been more confident of my own life's meaning.

I know nothing can be changed "back there." So to those of my generation I enthusiastically say, "It is never too late to find your place, your divine intention, your meaning. It is never too late to start painting wooden bowls or anything else your heart leads you to." To my children and to all who are young I say, "*Take* your time. Take *your* time. Take it better than I took mine. Look *now* for those opportunities and choices that will bring out your wonderful giftedness. Look for chances to create, not just work."

3) The Wonder of Influence and Opportunity

This third wondrous secret takes the baton from the second. Not only do I suggest that we are supposed to seek places of opportunity that welcome our giftedness and creativity, I believe that our entrance into them should literally change the world. As you seek your richly imagined meaningful future, look for opportunities that really *matter* and make a difference. You can have a situation in which your creativity and gifts are needed, but ask yourself: how will the world be richer because of it? If you can't see how, keep looking. You will not find meaning there.

The word "influence" means "to flow in," to truly and fully enter into life. I remember reading this wonderful quote: "Take the world as you find it, but don't leave it that way." Whoever said that understands this secret better than I. Change things! *If you can't change it, don't get involved.*

116

Bring new freshness and vitality to this parched world that has been so long in spiritual drought.

I get so tired of people wanting me to speak on "how to cope with change" or "how to manage change." Change is not a disease. It is the evidence of life! My friend and colleague Linda Tarrant gives a wonderful presentation titled, *"Change – the opportunity of a lifetime!"* I wish I had thought of that title. Our entire existence is about change. There is nothing more wonderful than to influence change. *Cope with* change? How about *hope for* change? Never mind *managing* change – *lead* change! It does not matter whether you are the Board Chairman of a Fortune 100 company or whether you clean up the place at night. Change something!

Your life matters! Everyday we are all meant to bring about wonderful and positive changes in our world. Don't let anyone convince you otherwise through their words or actions. If you are looking at choices that seem to imply that you should just fit in and not rock the boat, run the other way and look in a new direction. As you approach your chosen field and see a herd of sacred cows, take your wire cutters and set them free. The meaning of your life is measured by what you have changed.

4) The Wonder of Differences

Is there some sort of "diversity" program where you work? Diversity is a rather touchy and important issue in the corporate world today and it points to one of the secrets to a life of meaning.

I'm about to speak to a major Human Resources conference and, according to the program, there must be at least five concurrent sessions around this issue. Corporations have diversity departments, manuals filled with policies about diversity and managers whose job it is to ensure the acceptance of diversity. Many governments have actually implemented legislation to legally enforce diversity. *And,* should someone be found guilty of not appreciating diversity, they are sent to "diversity training." Can we really "train" people out of a racist or sexist or some other discriminatory attitude? I won't bet on it. What we end up doing is "training" them not to say or do certain things that will get them, or us, sued. That may be a start, but it doesn't reach a narrow and self-centered heart.

At first read, this may sound like I am against such initiatives. Exactly the opposite is true. However, what is terribly sad is that we treat the non-acceptance of each other's differences as an occurrence that can be resolved by political and intellectual intervention. Failure to accept the wonder of differences is first and foremost a *spiritual* problem. It will *never* be overcome with legislation or training.

Our differences, of course, cover the whole gamut from our racial backgrounds to our gender, height, weight, religion, how we prefer to clothe ourselves, how we process information, how we eat and our age as well as to our physical abilities. Each variable we can think of adds more rich depth to the tapestry. Do we joyfully and gratefully revel in these distinctions? Rarely. Most of the time we try to tolerate them, hoping we don't do something stupid that makes headlines. We play the politically correct game while we save our true feelings for private conversations held in elevators and parking lots.

A big step up from tolerating differences is to actually understand them. On this level we want to know and *understand* what it's like to have a disability or disfigurement. We want to know why Hindu men have to wear the mandeel around their heads. We listen again with more open ears and hearts to the story of what happened in Alabama in the sixties and what is still happening in many of our cities today. We'll take the time to learn why eastern music is different than western and why it is that we like one over the other. Of course, an even higher step up from "understanding" would have us actually *enjoying* our differences. Dr. Fons Trompenaars, arguably the world's leading authority on cross-cultural matters, suggests that the ultimate level of dealing with differences is "reconciliation," which he defines as "resolving seemingly opposing values." Apply that intention to the tension in the Midddle-East, for example, and you have one enormous challenge.

An incredible and indefensible western conceit is often at play in cross-cultural differences. Even when westerners travel to someone else's country, the attitude is that others don't quite come up to standard. Many times in my travels I have overheard North American tourists muttering in the most condescending way about "these people" and why can't they do this or that. "Why can't they think, act and look like us?" is what is really being asked. While eating dinner in a restaurant in Mexico, I overheard the gentleman next to us ask the waiter for a glass of water. Without a blink the waiter said, "Would tomorrow be okay?" It took the man a moment to realize the waiter was just joking and playing off a stereotype. My honest opinion is that if people don't want to experience other cultures, what they eat and how they do things then they shouldn't travel! Where this "God's gift to the world" attitude comes from I don't know. This self-adulation reflects a poor and starving spirit. It reflects weakness, not strength.

Perhaps if we could see God in all those to whom we feel superior, we might not feel so superior. As we seek to uncover our own divine intention, may we not run from differences but rather see them as the colors on God's palette. They are the colors that will brighten our own lives.

Why is this an important secret to your search for a meaningful life? We seldom stop to think that our differences are essential to the identification of our own meaning. If you and I are exactly alike, one of us is unnecessary. If all the paintings in your local art gallery are exactly the same, no one will go to see them and they won't be worth a nickel. Your meaning is found in what is *different* between you and your co-participators. The more diversity or differences you are reconciled to, the more significant is the meaning of your life. Find your Self among those who are different than you.

5) The Wonder of Pain and Forgiveness

Life hurts. Our bodies hurt. Our relationships hurt. Other people hurt us and we hurt them. And just to make sure there is enough pain in the world, we hurt our "Selves." Billions of co-participators are zinging all over our external and internal universes like atoms in a particle accelerator. Why are we surprised that there are collisions? Maybe what we don't understand is how the pain of collision can be a secret leading to a life of meaning. The purpose here is not to launch into a further explanation of why bad things happen to good people, or even to bad people for that matter. The wonder of pain is that it can serve as a beacon to bring us back to where we need to be. Therein lies the power of the secret. Joy can do that too – but we listen better to pain.

120

If I have heart murmurs and constant shortness of breath I may finally drop the thirty pounds I need to lose. If there is a silent tension in a relationship that I value, I may be drawn to examine how I treat him or her and consequently save or even strengthen the relationship. If the quarterly results of my business are so low that I slump in my chair, maybe I'll finally smarten up and get focused and organized. If I pay attention to soreness in my shoulder I may go for the physical I haven't had in eight years. If I cough up blood, maybe I'll finally quit smoking and thereby save my own life and stop damaging the lives of those around me. If I experience the pain of being laid-off at work I may seize the opportunity to start the business I've always dreamt about. If someone dear to me dies, I may begin to attend to the things that are truly important in life. If I wake up in an alley in an alcoholic daze, still dressed in my business suit with my briefcase clutched in my hand, maybe I'll have hit bottom sufficiently hard that I'll start to get up. If one of my kids has managed to get himself into a jam, I may stop and rethink how I am fulfilling my role as a parent.

Got the idea? Good. Now let me say that all of this flows easily off the keyboard because I am not in pain right now. If I were in pain, the above would probably have been a very different paragraph. When we are in the middle of the pit, having someone point out the "wonder of pain" is hardly welcomed.

If you *are* in the pit of pain, my best advice is to *not* spend your limited energy trying to figure out the "why?" of your painful experience. Most of us don't have that degree of spiritual insight. I know I don't. Instead, spend your energy keeping your eyes, mind and heart open to what is available to you in the experience. Deal with the issues as they come before you. Ask forgiveness when you need to. Give forgiveness when you have the opportunity. Listen to the feedback your world is giving you. Accept help from those you trust and who care about you. Make the choices you need to make as best and as honestly and as wisely as you can. *Then,* when you can see the dawn of a new day and have the time and energy to reflect, you can start to ask, "Now, what did those wonders mean?" and the secret will begin to have its effect.

In no way am I saying that pain is something to be enjoyed; that would be like sado-masochism for the soul. What I am pointing out is that, on the far side of pain (and may that far side be very near for you if you are in pain right now) you are able to look back and see what wonders that pain brought into your life.

I'll give you some examples of what I'm getting at. Your spouse took ill suddenly. Actually that is a bit of understatement; she was in intensive care for nine days and it was touch-and-go for a while. The truth was that the relationship between the two of you had cooled noticeably over the last few years and, while there was no animosity, there was no romance either. But one late evening as you sat there watching the drip drip drip of the intravenous and the neon blips on the monitor, your eyes began to give up the tears they had held for so long. She is precious, you thought, as you took her hand. As you whispered, "I do love you honey," through your tears, at that very moment a renewed commitment was born. Never again would you take her for granted and never again would you waste a single day of this wonderful gift.

"Right. Give it a month after things are back to normal," the most cynical among us will think. He may be right, of course, but does that lessen the presence of a wonder? A second chance has been given whether or not you act on it. Am I recommending a visit to death's door as a therapeutic tool? Not for a moment. Indeed I wish you the wonder of health. However, I am saying that the experience of pain *can* lead us to life-changing discoveries.

Sometimes you can see the guiding power of pain more easily in others. For example, your youngest brother, having managed to graduate from high school, is in a job he hates. Not only is it menial, unexciting and poor paying work, he is on the night shift three weeks out of four. You know the entire family has been on his back about what he should do and what further education he needs because you have led those discussions. But the most effective strategy is probably to let pain reveal its secret. The pain will speak louder and louder until one day he listens and makes his own choices.

Or how about this one? Your company's share value has dropped like a rock in just one quarter. The downturn is not easily explained to your Board, your shareholders or your employees. In the rush to stop the bleeding, you discover that there is incredible internal warfare between you and your distribution agents. They have spread the word that they will not be supporting your product line unless the quality and compensation improves. Why it has taken three months for this message to get to you is an interesting question you can answer later. Remember – don't worry about figuring out the "whys?" of it all until you've got the time, energy and perspective. Right now you initiate an emergency agent–vendor task force to get the problems sorted out. First, it's a wonder that you are still in business. Second, this *pain* has pushed you into rethinking your relationship to your agents and will, in due course, push you into reexamining the communication lines in your own company. Wonderful! The only sad thing is that these "messages" from your universe were there all along; you just didn't see or hear them. They had to slap you on the head to get your attention. Like I say, pain is a good motivator.

Pain, like anger, can draw us to significant and much-needed choices. Pain can tell us we are too self-centered, married to the wrong person, in the wrong job, eating the wrong food, or drinking too much. If we listen to pain's message, a wonder has happened and the secret has done its job.

And what about "forgiveness?" Human beings are capable of inflicting incredible damage to one another's *person*, to one another's *Self*. Nothing is more painful than a wounded soul. When we inflict pain on another's *Self*, we are acting as though that person did not exist. We talk about that person as though he were not here and criticize him as though he did not feel. When it happens to us, we might say to the one who has hurt us, "I don't think I even *matter* to you!" I'm sorry to say that you are *only* matter – a "thing" that cooks and cleans, or brings in extra income, a sex object or a means for social acceptability. But to all human intents and purposes, you don't exist as a person to the one who has taken and damaged your Self.

In some cultures you can literally dismiss someone out of your life. You might deny the person's very existence by declaring, "To me you are dead!" And presto, as far as you are concerned he *is* dead. In North American culture we do much the same thing in our relationships all the time; we are just not so clear about it. How awful that one person can damage another in this way.

The reality is that this has happened to me, and it has probably happened to you. When someone for-*takes* your Self this way it is very hard to for-*give* them for doing so. Ironic isn't it? To get your Self back, you have to give even more to the one who has taken it. But that is what for*give*ness is – giving to those who have taken. When you witness true forgiveness, you witness a wonder of indescribable proportions. May you create such a wonder often throughout your life.

Here is how this secret can point you more clearly to your life's meaning. Look at where you are experiencing pain in body, mind, heart or soul and ask yourself what choices are being put before you. It is very likely that the choices you see you will have known about for some time but have not responded to them. Secondly, look for opportunities to *forgive* those who have hurt you – you will be amazed at what you will get back.

6) The Wonder of Joy and Congruence

On the far side of pain is a most wonderful secret – the wonder of joy. Joy is the evidence that life makes sense, if even for just a moment. How many moments can I put you down for? Experience enough joy-full moments and you'll have a whole day full of joy. String enough days together and you'll have one joy-full week. A joy-full year? One can barely imagine it. Indeed, perhaps we are not meant to imagine it. Perhaps we do not really *want* to be joy-full which is why we can't imagine an ongoing state of joy.

I really don't know why joy is so illusive. But if joy is contingent on knowing our richly imagined future, the meaning of our life, maybe a lot of us are in trouble. In *A World Waiting to be Born*, M. Scott Peck estimates that only five to ten percent of the population has a sense of destiny, and that is, one's specific and grand personal purpose. Does this mean that if ninety to ninety-five percent of us don't know our destiny, we also don't have joy? If this is really the case, finding joy in our lives is almost on the level of winning a lottery. Maybe it *is* all about luck.

What convoluted thinking is going on here? We get two short paragraphs into a discussion on joy and some form of pessimism starts creeping in and ruins it all. Why would we, why would *anyone,* not want joy? If having joy means that our life is making sense, then of course we want all we can get. So how come, in her wonderful book *Light Dances,* Shirley Trout sadly comments that, "youth appear to find woefully few adults who demonstrate any joy in being alive?" How come poet David Whyte, in his spiritually rich book, *The Heart Aroused,* insists that the experience of joy is incredibly rare, particularly in the workplace?

Whyte seems to suggest that our problem with joy is exactly what has happened in these first two paragraphs on the subject. We see joy coming toward us and we do something to it or to ourselves that allows us to escape from its embrace. It is like the crotchety pessimist who is finally talked into going to a New Year's Eve party, almost starts to have a truly good time, and then catches himself. The retirement subdivision where my parents live has a sign near the main gate: "Population 2,723 and one grouch." We all know the person who seems to have dedicated his life to misery. If one could become joyful by breathing, he would hold his breath. Here is how Whyte puts it: "...we may actually experience joy as a moment of terror. It opens to us all our possibilities and yet casts a shadow of comparison across all our other moments. Joy brings an intimation of death and mortality. This joy will pass as all others have before them."

Every parent has, at some point, given their children the warning: "Don't get your hopes up too high!" I guess if your hopes are too high there is more potential for disappointment. Of course that begs the question about what altitude hopes *should* be set at so as to avoid the pain of a fall. After all you can hurt yourself stepping off a curb. Or what about the adult person? You are reveling in the loving joy of a new German Shepherd puppy and your neighbor tells you about an adult dog that tore apart the entire house and all who lived within it. You win a million dollars in a lottery drawing and can now pay for your mother's heart transplant when a friend (mis)informs you that 43% of all lottery winners commit suicide. Even the television weather person gets into the act. "Most of the nation can expect beautiful weather at the start of the week," she'll say, and then adds – in case you were starting to pack a picnic – "let's hope it lasts." The intimation, of course, is that it won't and you will probably spread your picnic blanket over a patch of poison ivy. Why couldn't she have said, "The weather for most of the nation is beautiful – *in-joy* it!"

How can we learn to *in-joy or joy-in* the experiences of life?

Here is how I think joy works. When we sit down to eat an absolutely incredible meal – one that sparkles in our eyes, flirts with our nostrils, rumbas with our tongues – we experience the joyous stimulation of all our senses. The actual process of chewing and swallowing is not particularly attractive so we won't dwell on it. Just note that, following along with the joy of taste, smell and so on, comes the strengthening assimilation of that food into our body. What began as sheer sensual joy now nourishes us. It literally becomes part of who we are. Likewise, when we go through

127

an experience that affirms our worth as a unique and royal creation, one that brings delight to our path, we are strengthened in our soul. If our food shapes us physically, our joy shapes us spiritually.

Now here is where the metaphor becomes a little more complicated. When we eat, the consumption and digestive process has many components to it, each essential to the value and purpose of eating. However, some of these components are highlighted for our undivided and joyful attention while others are just there and we don't even think about them, let alone rejoice in them. At the restaurant I doubt that any of your dinner companions will sigh, "Oooo I just love it when my food goes into my intestines!" or "There is nothing more wonderful than when my stomach acid begins to decompose my food." (If they do, you need to get some new friends – and I mean *now*!) Some aspects of our experiences we label "joyful" and other aspects we don't label at all; they are just there. We label the sizzle of the steak but we don't label its decomposition in our stomachs. Still it is important to remember that *all* aspects are essential to the whole experience of joy. When we don't see it this way there is the tendency to denigrate the more mundane and less exciting aspects, or even become angry at them. The point is, not all parts of joy need to be euphoric in order to be part of joy.

Finally, let's go back to the point Whyte makes, that we reject joy because we are afraid we will lose it. If you never fall in love you don't run the risk of having your heart broken. Of course you *do* run the risk of having no heart at all. This is common thinking. If you can avoid joy, you will avoid the pain of losing joy. But, I can't imagine sitting at a restaurant table and saying, "I don't think I'll eat this incredible meal because tomorrow's dinner may not be as good." The secret to full life is *Carpe Joy*! Eat while it's hot! Be nourished now – it will make you stronger for whatever tomorrow brings.

To tell you the truth, because I travel a lot speaking at corporate events, I get to eat in some pretty nice places. After a week of this forced indulgence, eating a bowl of mac n' cheese at home while watching reruns of M*A*S*H in my underwear starts to look pretty good and usually proves to be just as joyful an experience.

I am suggesting that evidence of joy is an indicator that you are on track to finding a life of meaning. I am *not* suggesting that just because every single thing doesn't bring ecstasy you are *off* track. The wonder of joy points to an emerging congruence in your life's direction. When we learn to *joy-in* the choices that make up our lives, we will also have the wisdom to know with which of the options available to us we are to *joyn*. Let's make "joyn" a new word that means to become part of something with enthusiasm, energy, zest and celebration. The happy sixth secret is that meaning will be found in those circumstances that bring delight to your soul. Joyn in with everything you've got!

7) The Wonder of Knowing

There is no question that we know almost immediately when our lives are *not* in alignment, when something just *isn't* right. We get restless, irritable, angry. Doesn't it make sense, then, that we'd also know when our lives *are* in alignment? The universe graciously gives witness to the rightness of our path when we are honed in on our richly imagined future. One voice of this witness is the inner sense of knowing. Here we tackle the most mysterious secret of all.

Though I must, I regret throwing in a caution right at the outset of this wonder. My concern is that any caution will minimize the validity and power of the gift of simply *knowing* things. You noticed that I said *knowing* is only one of the voices that tell us we are on the right course toward our richly imagined future. If we weren't all so human, it would be the only voice we need. But, unfortunately, foibles like selfishness, greed, lust, jealousy, impatience and pride have an uncanny ability to disguise what we *want* as what we *know*. The two are not always synonymous.

We can see this most clearly in our children because their *knowing* gift has not matured. For example, while out shopping for a jacket for your six year-old daughter, she spots one with "Barbie" in sequins on the back. This jacket is *so* cool. "Honey," you say, "that jacket won't fit you." "Yes it will. I *know* it will!" she insists, her divine *knowing* sense contaminated by the intense carnal desire to have.

Have you ever bought a car you wanted desperately but couldn't afford? Do you remember the mental machinations you went through to get yourself to the point of "knowing" that was the right decision to make? In case you are not good at the justification game, here are a few of my best machinations. "It always pays to buy quality and in the long run this car will be a much wiser investment than some sedate sedan." "If you look successful, you will be successful." Or how about, "People want to deal with a winner and winners don't drive beat-up second-hand cars." If all else fails, combine the, "it's not for me, it's for you" technique with, "New cars today are so much safer than the old ones and I want that for you and the kids."

All such thinking is a contaminant to the wonder of knowing. And, let's 'fess up – we have all made many decisions in our lives that, if it hadn't been for greed, lust, gluttony, pride or any number of other human weaknesses, we would not have made. The path to true *knowing* is a rocky one indeed.

Wouldn't it be great to go through life with someone right beside you who "knows what's best?" Or would it? On second thought, it could be rather annoying and would probably take a lot of the fun out of life. Without the spiritual exercise of *trying* to know, this wonder would atrophy. Could it be that we are meant to struggle in our attempts to know? I think *knowing* is a wonder that gradually unfurls like a blossom, so that over our lifetime we slowly come to see the real beauty of the gift.

Yet we have all had multiple occasions in which we've made a choice about something only to have someone question the wisdom of that choice. "How do you know that's the right thing to do?" they question, hoping for logical and conclusive documentation of irrefutable evidence verifying your decision. "I *just know*." we respond, hoping there will be no more interrogation. If you are really emphatic you say, "I just *know* that I *know!*" That phrase is the Ace of Spades of decision-making. How does one trump it? Replying, "No you don't" is not a very effective retort.

There is the old story of the church board meeting at which the deacons were arguing over a particular expenditure. Finally one elderly deacon rose to his feet and said, "I prayed long and hard about this decision last night and God clearly told me that we should go ahead with this decision." On the opposition side an even older deacon rose with equal righteousness and stated, "I talked to God just this morning, and he said, 'cancel all previous communication!'" If our human natures didn't muddy things up so much maybe we *could* know what God "thinks" is best.

"How do you know there is a God?" I *just know*. "How do you know she's the woman for you?" I *just know*. "You have a perfectly good job, why are you changing careers?" I *just know* it's the right thing to do right now. "How did you know you shouldn't get on that flight that crashed?" It was strange – somehow I *just knew* I shouldn't get on. How grateful we should be that, in spite of our self-seeking ways, somehow the *knowing* finds its way into our consciousness.

Unfortunately, though this is the seventh secret that will lead you to a life of meaning, I do not have a secret way for you to always *know that you know*. It has always been a struggle for me to be really sure as to what decision is truly in keeping with my richly imagined future. I'm sure that must be true for most everyone. What I try to do is be brutally honest with myself about my motivation for making certain decisions. I ask myself questions like, "What excites me most about this decision?" If the answer is that it only means more money or more publicity, I try to slow myself down in order to really reflect on what I am doing. Believe me – I am all for more money and publicity. But, somewhere deep inside, I *know* that if that's what my life becomes, I will soon be destroyed. Things like greed, pride, revenge and ego are the "viruses" of our lives. They are extremely hard to get rid of and not much, short of prayer, the tough-love support of friends and family, a little reflection and a few whaps on the head, provides adequate virus protection.

But if you think those contaminants are tough, you ain't seen nothin' until you've experienced lust! And we have *all* experienced lust. This is the mother of all viruses. Sexual lust will bring down more powerful people than any other force in the universe. Why is this so? The closest that I can come to an answer is the observation that providing leadership is a weighty and exhausting function. It is usually accompanied by constant criticism and challenge and sometimes comes without much reward. "If I, as a leader, can command the people and things around me," goes the internal rationalization, "surely I can command my own pleasure! Surely I deserve it." The more powerful and prominent one is, the more powerful and prominent is this delusion. While Presidents Kennedy and Clinton are textbook cases of this point, we see it everywhere from religious leaders to sports heroes. The late Wilt Chamberlain claimed to have slept with over 20,000 women. How did he keep count? On less notorious and energetic levels we see it in ourselves, that is, if we are willing to admit it.

Due to ego and self-righteousness, some people do not have the honesty and courage to declare themselves "human" in this regard. I was secretly pleased when *Hustler* publisher Larry Flynt offered a million dollars to anyone who could provide proof that politicians besides Bill Clinton had had extramarital affairs. There was so much phony self-righteousness flooding the corridors of power during President Clinton's difficulties that politicians lost virtually all credibility. The whole sad story taught us once again that the strong and powerful are the most vulnerable of all.

I can describe the wonder of these seven secrets, suggesting to you that they are the signposts to destiny. But can I actually tell you what your destiny is? Not in a thousand years. Can a vocational test point you in the direction of your divine calling? No. All it can do is point you to a job category. So how then are you or I to know? Let the secrets point you to the wonders. No matter what fork in your life's road you come to – take this job or start your own business; marry this person or opt to stay single; remain in this country or live overseas; go back to school or keep working – look at the wonders. These are your secret signposts.

Ask yourself, which of my choices most:

1) presents me with a situation in which love is most evident and where family is held sacred?

2) invites and encourages the discovery and use of my giftedness by giving me a chance to create something new?

3) wants and needs me to help change the situation?

4) exposes me to all of the colors in God's palette and celebrates the differences and diversities within creation?

5) closely reflects the outcome of the pain and difficulties of my life and will test my willingness to forgive those who have hurt me?

6) invites me to "joyn" with a spirit of joy, enthusiasm and celebration?

Finally, as you guard against the contamination of greed, selfishness, ego, revenge, lust and a host of other very human viruses, ask yourself:

7) What does my heart and spirit *know* to be the way for me?

Not all of the wonders will have equal impact on every decision point. Still, it generally remains true that when you see and experience any of the first six secret wonders you should go in that direction. As you do, you will experience the seventh wonder of knowing. And nothing in the world is as wonders-full as knowing you have found your purpose, your richly imagined future, your life's meaning.

Moving beyond our current reality toward our richly imagined future is a journey well worth taking. That does not mean it's an easy one, since we cannot move to a new place until we are prepared to leave the old place. This is a major transition requiring considerable disruption. The best choice you can make is to *self*-disrupt, rather than wait for the world to disrupt you. This is the challenge we face next. It is time to climb back down the mountain.

What Is the Meaning and Purpose of My Life?

You can find the answer to the most difficult question in the Universe.

ACTION FIVE

What would you like to richly imagine? At the end of this paragraph, put the book down and close your eyes. See yourself going into a beautiful house that contains a very long wall. The house is the created universe and this wall is your life, an essential and invaluable part of that universe. Hanging on that wall you see various pictures reflecting your life's imaginings, each one focused on a different dimension of your life. Some of these beautiful pictures may be about your family, a relationship, your career or workplace, or your education. As you scan the long length of this wall, do you notice any spaces where no picture is hanging? Maybe there is a picture but it is out of focus or you just don't like the way it looks hanging there. These gaps, and these distorted, and disliked pictures, need to be filled, clarified or replaced.

Your Assignment

To keep this reflective exercise manageable, write down only one or two of these dimensions of your life. You might use labels like "my marriage," "my job," "my teenage daughter" or "my health." Picking one at a time, begin to richly imagine the future you long and yearn for. *Now hold on for just a second.* If you are at all like me, you will immediately begin to inventory what you *don't* want in that future which means you are imagining negatives, shortcomings, fears, guilt, self-depreciation or whatever. Thoughts like "I wish there wasn't so much competitiveness in my marriage," and "There's got to be a job out there that is actually enjoyable," are familiar examples. You can see obvious negative implications in such statements. This is not a good start. So back up to where you walked into the beautiful house and look down that wall again.

This time, when you go to richly imagine your future, keep the seven secrets in your mind. They are: the wonder of *love and family*, the wonder of *giftedness and creativity*, the wonder of *influence and opportunity*, the wonder of *differences*, the wonder of *joy and congruence*, the wonder of *pain and forgiveness*, and the wonder of *knowing*. Use these wonderful secrets as an "imagining guide."

For example, if you yearn for a richly imagined future for your teenage daughter, grasp within that image how *love and family* would fit in. Imagine her discovering and using her giftedness and creativity in *influencing* the world through new *opportunities* that will surely come her way. See her being loved and treasured for who she is, for her *differences*. And, of course, see her value you for your differences. See the increasing *joy* in her life gradually pointing toward her divine purpose. Obviously, you will not want to imagine *pain* for her, but you can imagine triumph over the inevitable difficulties that will come along. Finally, frame this picture with the wonderful confidence of *knowing*.

Once you put these richly imagined pictures of your future together you can send them out into the Universe at will. The Universe is waiting for the delivery of your imaginings and it will immediately get to work on them.

137

Chapter Six

UNLEASHING YOUR POWER

E very one of us has been created with a divine intention. We are all created for a life of meaning. Unfortunately, the majority of us never hear the directions to this intention that our soul has been calling out since the moment we took our first breath. "Turn left here!" it has shouted, and we turned right toward the brighter lights. "Do not fear being laid off," it has comforted, "there will be a new and better opportunity very soon." We chose anger and depression rather than trust. "Talk to the person beside you on the plane," the voice whispered, and we chose to watch the movie instead. "He is not the partner for you," it pleads, but we gave in to sexual intoxication. "Do not doubt yourself," assures the voice, "apply for graduate school." Rather than take the risk, we spend the next twenty years telling everyone we are *thinking* of applying to graduate school. "You cannot afford that house," warns our soul. Our eyes clouded by visions of grandeur, we leap into bankrupty. Who among us hasn't ignored the clear voice within and suffered the consequence?

Why are we so hard of hearing? Why does it take us so long to learn? For one thing, we are almost totally consumed and distracted throughout our lives by the bump and grind of other co-participators. Secondly, and to an even greater extent, we are pummeled by the demand for compliance from the institutions to which we have plighted our troth. The predictable result is that we find ourselves actually in a "plight." We're being made to *comply* when what we desperately want to do is *commit*. Compliance is enforced by power external to our selves, whereas commitment is powered from within. Among the meanings of "commit" are "to begin" and "to assign." It is that inner knowing voice that tries to get our lives to begin our intention.

The tension between our intention and our institutions creates irritation. Rather than regarding our irritations as a pathology that needs to be "fixed," we can learn to use them to bring us back to our right path. Such course corrections do not happen automatically and they certainly don't happen easily. Four considerations can help.

1) The first is the admonition to understand our current reality and then to let it go. To dwell on our past is to repeat it.

2) The second is to revel in our richly imagined future, that wonderful clarity of purpose that seems to draw every aspect of who we are into line. We have found already, seven wondrous secrets that have the power to bring our life's meaning into focus.

3) The third consideration is about self-disrupting our lives and unleashing our power so we are free to change and grow.

4) The fourth is making courageous choices (which we will tackle in Chapter Seven).

We have all heard someone refer to another as being "filled with good intentions." Usually the phrase is used negatively, implying that that person's behavior is anything *but* "good." Somehow, it seems, a disconnect occurred between a laudable goal and the person's actions toward that goal. Ironically, the statement is actually a very positive truism. Most of us *are* filled with good intentions. So why is it that we can be willing to let go of the past, glue our eyes to the future, and *still* not go anywhere? I learned at least part of the explanation by watching corporations struggle to implement change, even positive desired change. I learned even more by watching my kids.

Most of us seem to function in predictable patterns. We wake to the same radio station at the same time each morning. We get the coffee machine percolating before we hit the shower. We sit at the foot of the bed to put on socks or nylons. We catch the 6:47 train and sit in the same car, same seat, every trip. We stop at Starbucks to buy a double latte grande decaf just before going into our office building. In the elevator we lean against the back left corner unless some other inconsiderate person is there first. We offer virtually the same greeting to our colleagues unless something truly unusual has happened the night before such as winning the office hockey pool. We check E-mails before we do anything else. And on and on. Were our days to be filmed, we'd have to classify much of our lives as "reruns."

The same thing happens in corporations. Over time certain patterns emerge. There's one for parking and one for cafeteria behavior. There is a pattern for decision-making and a pattern for producing performance reviews. It's the "how we do things around here" phenomenon. Sometimes this is even called "culture." I can't count how many times I've been contracted to help "change the culture" of an organization. That, in non-consultant language, is the same as being asked to "shake 'em up!" This always reminds me of a three-day conference on how to lead change in which the participants would have sat in exactly the same seats every day if I hadn't said anything.

Recently, I was with a senior leadership team of an insurance company. They were discussing how to lead their organization to even higher levels of performance and service. One observation was that many employees see something not working right during the course of their duties and yet they don't take any initiative to fix it. Just about the same time one of the hotel staff was pushing a cart with squeaky wheels down the hall. We had a great debate about how long we thought those wheels had been squeaking. My vote was for two years. If it's not in the pattern, it doesn't get done.

Situations like this reflect an ingrained pattern of behavior. The insurance company employees may not feel they are empowered to actually make decisions on their own. The hotel cart pusher may have a union contract that says he does not have to oil squeaky wheels. Who knows why we do or don't do things? The fact is if your life is a cookie cutter, you end up being a cookie. If your richly imagined future is to be a bagel, you've got a problem.

We must find a way to break the *mold*! You know, we human beings are great talkers. Every New Years Eve we babble through the bubbles about how we are going to do this and that. We're going to lose weight. We're finally going to quite smoking. We swear that we are going to get ourselves into some form of financial discipline. We attend a motivational seminar and immediately write out our short and long-range goals in the blanks provided on the speaker's handout and, at home, tape it to the fridge so everyone else can see how focused we are. Our company has its annual planning session and we are facilitated into covering large pieces of newsprint with revolutionary ideas and plans for change. We stand before our spouses and take our annual oath that we will finish the games room in the basement sometime before the Second Coming. What's the real, observable impact of all this talk? Virtually nothing. Many of us could kick ourselves for our inability, or unwillingness, to turn our talk into walk. Our motto is *grand parleur petit faiseur,* or all talk, no action.

It is even more annoying when others fail to deliver. At least *we* have good reasons for our failures. The man said he'd be there on Saturday between ten and noon to fix the air conditioning. You stayed home on the most perfect golf day of the decade for nothing. That lying weasel tried to tell you he meant *next* Saturday. What are you supposed to do until then – leave the fridge door open to cool off? This is the third time this month your beloved daughter has asked to borrow a hundred dollars from you and promises, "I'll pay you back next week Dad – don't you trust your own daughter?" If you could just see her delivering on her promise, you'd die a happy parent. Need I go on?

Why don't we deliver on our talk? We make good and right and essential plans that will be of immeasurable value to many others and *still* we don't deliver. It seems to be true in our personal lives as well as in our businesses. What is going on with us? *The Express on Sunday Magazine* once noted that the average person spends twelve years of a lifetime talking! I wonder how one could go about calculating how many years are spent *acting* on that talk.

I came to a point a while ago where I felt I just had to get some insight into this common reality. I was mostly interested in why corporations seemed to have such difficulty turning plans into action. At conference after conference, I'd exude to corporate audiences about the Promised Land that awaited them if only they had the vision. There was a Corporate Land, I'd say, flowing with milk and honey. This world of work lay just over the horizon. In it there was no pain or suffering, no political games or turf wars, no living or dying by quarterly results and no re-engineering. Only meaning, quality, service, customer loyalty and market share were present. As the conference theme music welled up to fill the ballroom, we watched the "happy snaps," joined hands in small groups, marveled in the security that only matching sweatshirts can bring and we *vowed* that this promised land was our new spiritual corporate headquarters. This was our time! We had the right stuff! We were the champions!

The euphoria would last no more than forty-eight hours, maximum. Two days from the point where the flames of passion and commitment were highest, someone in the company would make an arbitrary decision or circulate a caustic E-mail resulting in all bets being called off. The flight to paradise was canceled. "We knew it wouldn't last," the cynics would say about the spontaneous sprouting of team spirit. It hurts to say so, but you know what? They were right. Oh, we'd remember with fondness the last night around the piano bar, the time Norm fell into the pool during the formal Awards Night reception, and the pride that came with winning the "longest drive competition" on the eighth hole. But beyond that it was pretty well history. Newsprint goals? Gone. No one remembered to take them down and transcribe them. News of the innovative task forces that were set up with such enthusiasm? Well the Life Balance Committee had one meeting on Sunday afternoon but now it's not much more than a memory. Only the sweatshirts seem to last forever. About their yearly conference one executive said: "It's usually just an annual piss-up!" On another occasion the company President actually said in his "thank you" to me, "We know the effects won't last, but that was a great presentation!" Talk about milking the cow and then kicking the bucket over!

Most of my wardrobe has a company logo on it; I'm a walking fashion show of "who's who" in corporate America. Indeed, nothing makes me happier than to be speaking to a business audience about the meaning of work. Nothing brings me more joy than to help people pull back the curtains of their potential and show them the promise of the Promised Land. And nothing disappoints me more than to see people intellectually and spiritually ready for the journey only to have it called off by those most able to guide them on the way. I had to find out why this seems to happen so often.

Let me describe a familiar familial scene that led to some of my initial insights. Every family has been through the following scenario. It's a rainy Saturday morning. Your son (or daughter) is complaining about there being nothing to do. "What is there to do?" your child whines. "Surely you can find something in your room to play with," you respond, "I've spent more money on toys for you than my parents spent on me in my entire life! When I was your age I had to make my own toys!"

Finally, the child settles on a Lego set. An hour later he's made something, usually a weapon of war, thanks to the influence of American television and computer games. Proudly, he emerges to display his creation, explaining where the bombs go, how the wings fold back, where the pilot sits, and so forth. A good parent, of course, expresses overflowing admiration for such creativity, assuring him that someday he will be famous for his feats of aeronautical engineering. Watching the boy walk back to his bedroom, the parent is shocked that, in the wake of such praise, he is already taking the Lego structure apart. "What are you doing?" comes the anguished cry. "You just made it!"

Here is what kids know that we adults forgot long ago. Guess what Lego sets are for? They are as much for taking apart as they are for putting together! Want to know what many adults do with their figurative Lego pieces? They glue them! Never mind being figurative. I had told the Lego story at a conference on leadership when a man approached me at the break. Rather sheepishly, he offered this embarrassed confession. That past weekend he had helped his son build a Lego creation and then insisted that they actually glue it together. Not only did he ruin his son's Lego set – he also conveyed the message that rigidity and permanence are preferred over flexibility and creativity.

We see this everywhere. Once a policy has been adopted and put in the official manual, it will be there forever, regardless of its irrelevancy to a changing world. Once we select *our* pew in church, we'll sit in that same spot even if we have to be propped up at our own funeral. We glue our lives into patterns and routines and then wonder why nothing new and exciting ever happens to us.

Here's another example. A family finally completes a difficult jigsaw puzzle. For over a month this puzzle commands the dining room table. Guests must eat off their laps because of this puzzle. Do you know what the family does? They glue cardboard backing to the puzzle, frame it and hang it on a wall. Maybe I lack artistic taste, but it seems to me that, not only do they have a strange picture with dark squiggly lines all over it, they have destroyed the soul of its *puzzleness*.

Our routines and patterns are literal ruts in our brains. Fill in the ends of those ruts and you've got little graves signaling the stand-still of our lives. There may be an appearance of stability in glued Lego pieces, but there is also a surety of real danger. Our universe is constantly spinning and there is no way in which anyone or any organization can actually stand still. We are always moving toward life or toward death. On second thought, perhaps the best situation is to be moving toward both at the same time.

Here is the hard reality: *Either disrupt yourself, or the world will disrupt you.* We need to take our glued lives apart every once in a while so that we can create something new. If we wait for the universe to disrupt us, we will be at the mercy of those universal forces, some of which are not friendly.

Have you ever been in a situation so tense and unfulfilling that you say to yourself, "I've just got to get out of here?" That reaction is the soul crying out to be rescued from entrapment. At some point we all know that we are trapped in some form of spiritual, emotional or environmental cement and it is drying fast. We know it because we are angry, restless, depressed, irritable or just plain grouchy. And thank goodness for those signals, as unpleasant as they may be to you and everyone around you. This is the Fifth Secret you will recall. I don't remember ever meeting anyone who has not been in this position at some point. It is hard to be grateful for these "you're getting trapped" signals. But just as a muscle pain tells you to stop a particular exercise, so should these pains tell you to disrupt your life toward a state more conducive and nourishing to your true Self.

Sometimes, we are wise, and respond to these disruptive cues early on and by doing so manage to stay in control of our lives. The longer you wait the more likely it is you will give up your choices to some other person or force who may not have your best interests at heart. A few years ago I was in just such a restless state and I knew I had to do something to shake up my life. Frankly, this posed an interesting challenge for me. Where could I look to find some positive experience that would shake and disrupt me? I wasn't about to sign up for a weekend retreat about self-fulfillment, that was for sure. That environment was too familiar to be disruptive. Instead I started to look way out on the fringes of my comfort and experience zone.

Introduced to a small organization called Triquetra Journeys led by a wonderful and spiritual woman named Lorna Roberts, I decided to take a shamanic journey to the Amazon. This was not a typical tourist experience with participants lined up behind the guide, each having a matching jungle hat and a badge reading "HELLO my name is…" It was like living out *The Celestine Prophesy*. Here are the tamer portions of the journey's description from Lorna's brochure. *"This is a journey to the Amazon Rain Forest – a place that is acknowledged to be essential to the welfare of the planet. This journey must be approached with much respect – a razor-sharp balance is needed to not contribute to the jungle's further destruction, but rather to receive its nourishment and support its existence. We will be working with the master shaman Augustin Rivas, an expert in the plants and herbs of the jungle. We will spend twelve days at his healing site, Yushantaihita. It is about four hours by boat up the Amazon River from Iquitos and then a 1 1/2 hour walk into the jungle. Here the sense of removal from Western Civilization is immediately felt. We will study the healing and spiritual traditions of the Amazon in ceremony. We will be working with the principle of the 'dark feminine.' Unlike the spiritual disciplines that teach us to disconnect from the body, the principle of the dark feminine teaches deep reverence for the*

148

body as well as for the earth. The jungle with its moist fertility is an ideal place to meet this archetypal spirit. The focus of this journey is personal cleansing and transformation."

On the plane to Peru I read my preparation sheet. It informed me that, "*There are two fire ceremonies in the tradition of Shamanism, a 'fire purification' ceremony and a 'fire transformational' ceremony. The one that we are doing is the 'transformational' ceremony. It is traditionally done once a month on the full moon.*" All this not only sounded disruptive to me, it sounded almost frightening. What was a "dark feminine" for Pete's sake? And what did it mean to go through transformation by fire? I was entering into a situation where I had no experience and no skills, a situation where I had no option but to realize the talent that had brought me what acclaim and success I enjoyed was no longer useful. I didn't even know what I should or should not eat or touch. I didn't even know where it was safe to walk.

As beautiful as the jungle was, it was a hard trip. But what a powerful experience this turned out to be. "Unless you are fully serious about personal transformation, don't even think about signing up," I had been told. Was that advice right on target! On my return friends asked, "What did you learn?" I had no itemized intellectual answer for them. All I knew was that I had been moved to a different place.

That experience disrupted me. What would disrupt you? What would it take to bring you face to face with the context and choices of your life? What would make you take your Lego set apart and begin to build something fresh and wonderful? Not everyone has to run off to the jungle to get sorted out. Reading a book or seeing a movie might do it; so might having a long conversation with a friend who loves you. Maybe all it will take is spending a week by yourself at a cabin by a lake. I'd even like to think that some of my speeches have disrupted people to a better and happier life. I know that has been true on at least one occasion. A woman came up to me at a conference and said, "Since the last time I heard you speak I quit my job, left my husband and moved across the country." Fortunately she added, "And I've never been happier!" It simply takes the right situation, the right word, the right spirit, the right readiness to spark regeneration in a human soul. We are *all* magical. If we can touch and move the hearts and souls of people, we can touch and move the world.

The secret to the disruptive notion is that it is best if it is *SELF*- disruption. In other words, *we* see why we need to shake up our lives and *we* choose an experience that will allow and encourage us to make the desired changes. Do you remember, as a little kid, having a battle with your mother over who should take the old Band-Aid off your skinned knee? Which will hurt the most, you wondered, doing it yourself or having mom do it? For a six-year-old this was a serious medical debate worthy of attention from the Mayo Clinic. Tired of the argument, mom would rip it off your knee with the swiftness of a Ninja. The suddenness of it all was more frightening than anything else. The trick was to try and get your knee to bleed so she'd feel guilty for frightening you so. Maybe in the case of Band-Aids it's okay to have someone else do it, but when it comes to disrupting your life, do it yourself.

Sometimes we are not prepared to do so because we are stubborn or selfish. But know this: sooner or later, want it or not, you *will* be disrupted. Your brother's death from alcoholism will finally make you look at your own over-consumption. Your wife taking the kids and moving to her mother's place until you can decide if you are serious about the family will cause you sleepless nights trying to figure out where you went wrong. Your unhappiness at work will manage to get you fired. When your son is expelled from school you will start wondering who convinced you that the quantity of time spent with your child was not important. These are disruptions all right and though they can bring deep pain, they can also lead to something good. I've had my share of such "disruptions" imposed on me and, I've got to tell you, I wish there was an easier way to learn. Still, they always led me to a better place.

In *Going Deep*, I called these disruptions the "shudderings" of our lives, the events that shake us to our core. Because we live, for the most part, in a negative and angry culture, the assumption is that these disruptions and shudderings are always painful. Many of them are – but not all. Being part of the birth of our children is an incredibly disruptive and shuddering experience. But would you trade that memory for anything? Life just can't be the same after you have children and most of us wouldn't want it to be. Meeting and marrying Georgia was a major disruption for me, too. Again, because we are so conditioned to seeing disruption as a negative, it sounds like a strange thing to say. The wonderful fact is she changed my life and I wouldn't want it any other way. The more you are able to choose your own disruptions, the more likely they are to be wonderful and positive.

The principle of self-disruption is equally applicable to the organizations of our lives. We are constantly living under decisions, policies, rules, regulations, procedures and protocols that long ago lost their usefulness. In Venezuela you could end up in jail for three days if caught kissing in public. In Indiana it is against the law to sell a car on Sunday. Lollipops are banned in Washington. You are not allowed to take more than three sips of beer at a time while standing, according to a law in Texas. In Chico, California, there is a $500 fine for detonating a nuclear weapon within city limits. In 1997, a bill was introduced to the Tennessee Legislature that would prevent people from eating their household pets. It was defeated because they couldn't agree on the definition of "pet."

Our civic leaders seem able to make some very creative decisions. The thing to remember is that at the time these decisions were made, something happened to convince the "leaders" that a new law or policy was needed. Out came the political glue. Some of those reasons may even have had some legitimacy. But why, once a law is enacted, aren't these same leaders able to recognize when the situation has changed and the "law" has now become foolish? They are great at putting things in place but just about hopeless at throwing them out.

The same applies to corporate policies and procedures. Most organizations are currently operating under policies that long ago lost their usefulness. Think of it. How many times have you sat working on some mundane task and asked yourself, "Why am I doing this?" You know it's a waste of time. Your boss knows it's a waste of time. You'd think that would mean you could quit doing that task wouldn't you? Not so. I have heard people estimate that as much as 60% of their activities at work add no value whatsoever. I am reminded of the classic story of the man in Nigeria who for decades faithfully went out to the pipeline each morning to turn the valve on and at night went out to turn it off. After he died someone checked on what this valve actually did only to discover that neither end of the pipeline had ever been connected to anything. How fortunate for that faithful man that he never knew! What a breach that would have been to him. It is an enormous breach of our self-worth to realize that the work we are doing is pointless and without value.

People seemed to be really on edge at a conference I was conducting for a bank. Having recently been re-engineered, they were trying to do twice the work with half the people. "We don't have enough time," they complained. I told them they had all the time there is, though they did not appreciate that insightful humor. Trying to help out, I asked them to name something in their routine that they knew, beyond a shadow of a doubt, added no value whatsoever. Immediately half the group named a report they had to prepare once a quarter. They felt it was a total waste of the two days it took to get it ready, duplicated and distributed. Since the entire organization was present, I decided to tackle the matter right then and there. First I checked with the President. He didn't know what report we were talking about; certainly it was of no value to him. Other executives were familiar with it because it had been part of the bank's reporting system for some time. No one admitted to using this report. For many years the intention of the report had been fulfilled by more sophisticated online data reporting. "Given that," I said, "is there any reason any of us ever have to do or see this report again from this day forward?" The room was silent. "I declare it gone!" I exclaimed with a sweeping gesture as though I had just performed an exorcism. That simple and brief interchange gave back two days a quarter to those good folks so they could do something that was actually useful. Now what I want to understand is this. Why did I, as an outsider, have to be the one to instigate an "*un*doing?" Why didn't one of them, years ago, stand up at a staff meeting and say, "This report is absolutely pointless. Let's quit doing it." Think of all the time, money and aggravation that would have saved.

Real leaders create self-*disruption* – not *destruction*. Real leaders prune the corporate systems and culture for dead policies, procedures, regulations and protocol. Some will argue that the old irrelevant rules aren't doing any harm since no one follows them anyway. I think that is a mistake operationally and it certainly is one metaphorically. It is like keeping two years worth of old E-mail messages on your computer. They aren't exactly doing any harm per se, but they do slow things down and are constant reminders of days gone by. Clean things up and you will be amazed at the new creativity and growth that will follow.

Xerox Canada did an unusual and interesting thing a while ago. Space in headquarters was scarce and expensive, yet storage rooms were full of old stuff. In fact, *everybody's* office was full of old stuff. So one Saturday their president, Kevin Francis, ordered in pizzas and drinks and the entire staff, including executives, came in to throw out anything that was not useful anymore. As I recall, they threw out three or four dumpsters full of old files, binders and whatever. If this self-disruption was seen only as a demonstration that Xerox would not be tied to the past, it was worth it. And no, they did not make a copy of everything before they threw it out. These folks self-disrupted themselves to an incredibly successful future. You could just feel it.

If you encourage the people in your organization to seek out and remove irrelevant and debilitating policies and regulations you will be rewarded with an incredible increase of creativity and innovation. Chances are your organization has lots of them. If you took part in creating those policies and regulations, it may be difficult to recognize when they have lost their usefulness since you were the one who gave birth to them. To its mother every baby is beautiful. That's why you need the perspective of others. Think of it this way: that "child" is grown and gone and it's time to give birth to something new.

There is one more dimension of self-disruption that should be noted, particularly in the work place. Since we build and launch things with great fanfare, we need to signal their end with equal demonstration. People will not believe that the old policies are dead unless they attend the funeral. Do not self-disrupt quietly. Do it with flare and do it with fun. When you have identified aspects of the business that need to be undone, celebrate the passing. You might even remind people why that policy came into being in the first place and, if it's possible, physically remove that page from the binder. Make it a celebration just as you would in burning your home mortgage once it's paid off. If the deceased policy is computerized, delete it from the file and leave behind a humorous memoriam.

Self-disruption frees you from the past and prepares you to journey to a new place. Failure to do so is like setting out on a cruise but forgetting to untie the boat. You can have the motor running at full speed, feel the vibration, and see water churning out the back end but if you are still tied to the dock the scenery is not going to change until you untie your boat!

Still self-disruption only releases you from the past and does not, in itself, take you to a new place. To do that, we have to go one step further. Just as undoing must be accompanied by doing, freedom must be accompanied by commitment, memories must be accompanied by an imagined future, and a sense of destiny must be accompanied by choice.

What Is the Meaning and Purpose of My Life?

You can find the answer to the most difficult question in the Universe.

ACTION SIX

It's time to rip off the metaphorical bandage and deliberately disrupt your life. Despite the initial discomfort you will feel, once you get on to the idea of regular self-disruption, you will find more and more opportunities presenting themselves to you. Unless you plow up the ground, you will have no place to scatter the seeds of the Seven Secrets.

Your Assignment

Disruption can be disturbing. To edge us into it, we'll begin with fun stuff. Try a few of these ideas just for the heck of it.

- Sleep on the other side of the bed for a couple of nights.

- Cut your lawn in a different pattern.

- Go to a matinee at an East Indian or Chinese movie theatre.

- Find a totally different route to work on each of the next three days.

156

- Locate a friend from high school days who you haven't talked to for years and call him or her.

- Bid for something on e-Bay.

- Learn a few phrases in sign language.

- Register for a course in something totally out of character for you.

- Visit a tourist site in your area that you have never been to before.

- Go help out at the Food Bank or a place serving the homeless.

- Wear your watch on the other arm

You get the intent here. Just do something different! Once you disrupt your life in relatively minor ways, you will be ready to disrupt it more significantly. You will find yourself seeing the world from a totally new vantage point. And when that begins to happen, you will also see amazing new opportunities.

Now for the harder stuff – and even here we'll wade into it. Begin with work. This week, keep your eyes open for a policy, procedure or practice that you honestly feel has outlived its usefulness. Take the time to find out how that particular thing came into being, the original reason for it, who was behind it, what benefits it may have brought the company and so on. This sort of research will prevent you from focusing on something just because you don't like it. If you discover that this policy, procedure or practice truly no longer adds value to the company or its customers, set out on a crusade to change it. Keep in mind that the situation may be best served by not having this policy or procedure at all, or it may be that modification is needed to restore its relevancy to the current situation.

Once you have gone through a few minor disruptions, you may be ready for a real, self-induced "shuddering." What, in your life, do you think has become a "crutch" for you? Used in this way, a "crutch" is something you don't really need but you have become used to. That sounds innocent enough but in reality it is like being thirteen years old and still having the training wheels on your bicycle. They may have been a good idea until you got "the hang of it," but after that they hindered your development and you never learned to balance. A crutch is helpful after you have sprained your ankle, but if you don't start testing yourself without it, you will never gain back the strength you once had. What are your crutches?

In my early days of struggling to get my business going, credit cards were my crutch. Like most people starting their own business, I wanted the desk, the computer, the leather couch and the company car by the end of the first week. Wait until I could afford them? Are you nuts? Of course I couldn't afford all this stuff on my own, that's why I relied on the credit card crutch. That got me into some pretty tense moments when I was almost afraid to answer the phone in case it was someone looking for a payment.

So what do you need to disrupt? What has become a crutch for you? Not wanting to break your dependency on your parents? Smoking, eating or drinking too much? The fact that in seven years you'll be eligible for your pension? Your alimony income? Your workaholic behavior? Your tenure as a college professor? Your health problems?

Even in trying to list some examples for you, it strikes me that knowing exactly what is and what is not a "crutch" can be very difficult. Only *you* can know. *Do you often use this "thing" as an excuse for not doing something you know you are meant to be doing?* For example, you have always felt destined to explore a whole new area of learning in third world health issues, but you have a comfortable tenure at a university teaching sociology. Why should you give up that security to go and study something that may or may not prove fruitful? Or, you have learned that if you keep busy enough at work, you have an excuse for not developing any meaningful relationships. But the truth is, relationships and commitment frighten you. Your parents don't charge you rent and your mother still makes your lunch and does your laundry. Why would you give that up just because you are twenty-seven? What a tragedy it would have been if two-time Tour de France champion cyclist Lance Armstrong had said, "I'm sorry, but my testicular cancer has spread to my lungs and brain. I shouldn't ride any more." Could he have had a more reasonable excuse not to fulfill his destiny?

I encourage you to identify just one crutch, one factor, one circumstance on which you have been relying a little too much. Design a disruptive plan that will enable you to escape from it.

Some will protest that you should not have change "for change sake." Why not? It keeps you loose and ready to dance. Get used to shaking up your life a little. Who knows what you will discover!

Chapter Seven

MAKING
COURAGEOUS CHOICES

I once owned a cottage on a beautiful fresh water lake in northern Ontario. One summer I had a large and very heavy floating dock built for me by my friend Kim Dunford. You won't find a better wood builder anywhere in the world. Because he built this monster in his back yard we were going to have to truck it to the nearest part of the lake and then barge it across the bay. A number of us stood looking at the dock for a good half hour. We made good use of the time. First we discussed our "current reality" – how solidly it was built, how much material went into it, how we were going to keep it on the back of the truck, how long it would take to tow across the bay, and how heavy it was going to be. Especially how heavy it was going to be.

The rest of the time we spent on the "richly imagined future." We talked about how great it was going to be to have that much more decking out over the water, how wonderful it would be to have a slip to hold the boat securely, and how it should last a good fifteen to twenty years even if it was left in the ice during the cold northern Canadian winter. Oh could we imagine!

After what I thought was far too brief a discussion, Kim drawled, in his wonderful country way, "Well I guess it's not going to move by us just talking about it." That disrupted us back to reality very quickly. You know, not much does move just by talking about it, except, maybe, our lips. Sooner or later somebody has to *choose* to do something. Push a button. Pull a lever. Sign on the dotted line. Take a stand. Lift a very heavy dock.

What choices will you and I make to ensure that we are in line with our innate purpose, our contract with the universe? Everything in life comes down to a choice. Choice is what defines how we live. More than that, the *ability* to choose is the primary evidence that we are truly and fully alive. Whether we have the *opportunity* to choose is another matter that we will discuss as we go along. The ability to choose shows we are alive. The opportunity to choose shows we are liv*ing*. The "*ing*" is important because it denotes a current state of motion.

When someone writes a will they will often begin it with that wonderful phrase, "Being of sound mind…" I'd love to be of sound mind one of these days. This is a way to let everyone know that the person is perfectly capable of making choices about what will happen to his estate after he dies. He has the *ability* to do so and he is taking advantage of the *opportunity* to do so.

To be crystal clear about how choice points first to life and beyond that to living, consider two populations for whom real choice is *not* an option. I had considerable dealings with the first group back when most of my consulting work was focused on the health care field. Particularly in long-term care facilities, I'd often see folks who, because of advanced age or some mental or physical disabling factor, appeared no longer able to make choices for themselves. This population had nothing to say about when they were bathed, when and what they were fed, or where they were placed to sit for the day. I'd see "sunrooms" filled with these good folks propped up in front of a common television. I go crazy if I don't have the remote in my hand, so I can just imagine what it must be like to sit there for hours tied to a chair watching goodness knows what. Who gets to choose the channel in these places remains one of institutional healthcare's most closely guarded secrets. And so they sit, measuring what is left of life only by the advent of the next meal. No wonder some of these dear people repeat over and over that they "just want to die." We hear that and we think how awful that wish is. It is a sad reality that there will come a day when many of us will understand it completely. When choice is gone so is the joy of living.

Here is the moral and medical dilemma facing health care professionals. How does one really know when someone has lost the *ability* to make choices for themselves? And as long as the person has some ability, shouldn't he or she be extended the respect of opportunity? All too often care givers decide that the ability is no longer there when the choice that that person would make, if given the opportunity, runs against the institutional rules. So if old Mrs. Robinson wants to make a choice to go for a walk in the garden, and truly has the *ability* to make that choice, she may find the *opportunity* is missing. The nursing home, short of staff and afraid that she may fall if she goes on her own causing her sons who run the law firm of Robinson & Robinson to sue, insists on enforcing Institutional policies which prevent that choice being made. Remember those Institutions from Chapter Two? They will be with Mrs. Robinson until the day she dies. Our Institutions will be with us until the day we die, too. We cannot fully escape them.

Should Mrs. Robinson be strong enough to fight the system and try to go for a walk anyway, she is likely to be sedated or, at the very least, a new policy will be put "into force" requiring the door to the garden be locked at all times. In this way the Institution can now claim that not only does she not have the *ability* to go for a walk, but also that policy does not give her the *opportunity* either, and *that's* why she is confined to the sunroom.

Unfortunately, when we do not give people who have the ability to make choices the opportunity to do so, they soon lose the ability as well. Both ability *and* opportunity atrophy and eventually disappear.

The other population I referred to experiences a similar dilemma. I'm talking about prisoners who are in jail because they made bad and hurtful choices sometime in the past. The most painful component of punishment for those convicted of breaking the law is that their choices are taken away. The worse they were at making choices, the fewer the choices they get to make now. "Maximum Security" provides fewer choices than "Minimum Security." The electric chair provides only two choices: your last meal and your last words. Even the warden's emphasis on the word "last" is a form of punishment because it highlights the reality that this life is literally down to its last couple of choices. We can't imagine how that must feel. Surely nothing feels more desperate than knowing you have run out of choices. It is not much of a life when choice is taken from you and it's not much of a choice when your life is taken from you.

Prisoners still have an *ability* to make choices but have had much of the *opportunity* to do so removed. Remember, a degeneration of opportunity sooner or later leads to a degeneration of ability. This is why some long-term prisoners find themselves unable to adjust to a life of choices on the "outside."

And the limitation of choice in prison impacts more people than just the prisoners. A psychologist friend of mine once studied why there was so much tension and stress among prison guards. Most people think it's because of the risk and danger. The primary source of stress that he found was boredom. Choice-less environments are not fun to live in, die in *or* work in.

Sometimes being *forced* to make choices can be a form of punishment. Just before the 1999 college football season two Florida State football players were caught stealing clothes from a men's shop. Part of their punishment included taking a course in "decision-making." Assuming the course was serious and meaningful, these two guys could learn to make wise choices now – or end up not being able to make any later.

When you think about it, we use the allocation and withdrawal of choice as our primary guidance tool in child rearing. Parenting, at its loving best, is the wise transfer of choice to the child. With an infant, very few choices are delegated by the parent. However, the infant is quite able to let the parent know when she is uncomfortable, whether she prefers pureed peas or carrots and when she wants to be picked up. As a consequence, while she herself may not actually have choices, she can insist that choices be made by her parents. She is very able to influence the direction of those choices. Who will get up for her midnight feeding? Who will change her?

A few years later, a five-year-old can be allowed to choose her clothing for the day, occasionally what she wants for breakfast, and which toys she'll take to Grandma's. But she does not get to choose where to go on the family holiday. She just does not yet have the *ability* to make that choice wisely and so is not given the *opportunity*.

To discipline our thirteen-year-old for coming home after her curfew, we "ground her" by removing some of her social choices for two weeks. As parents we know she is still in the process of developing her *ability* to make wise choices in the difficult context of other kids making their choices. We use the regulation of *opportunity* as the "check and balance" of child rearing. When she shows mature ability, we provide more opportunity. When immature ability is her choice, we restrict opportunity.

Some parents transfer choice to a child far too quickly and others far too slowly. For example, a misdirected dad might be proud that his fourteen-year-old son "can drink beer like a man." The boy does not have sufficient ability to handle the opportunity to drink extended to him by his father. While young teens have unhindered access to handguns and automatic rifles, they lack enough ability to handle them. The opportunity to get even by shooting up their school is just too much. By "ability" I don't mean how to aim and shoot accurately, I mean the maturity to make responsible choices. Most kids are just not ready for this level of choice when it comes to firearms. And yet *USA Today* reported that 40% of American homes with children have guns. One quarter of those guns are kept loaded. Opportunity without ability can become life-threatening.

Many parents worry that their children are being taught sex education at school at far too young an age. The parents think that such discovery will put choices before them they didn't even know existed, like deliberately putting youngsters into temptation's way, or showing them *opportunity* they didn't know they had. Sex educators, on the other hand, say that even very young children are being faced with sexual choices everyday and that education is one way to help them deal with that responsibility. Sexual opportunity is there already, the educators insist. And to a very large degree, children's sexual choices aren't in the parent's hands anyway. All parents can do is to lovingly and firmly teach and demonstrate solid values for their kids – and it's *never* too early to do that – and then pray. For most kids these days, *opportunity* greatly exceeds *ability*. As parents we have the ability and opportunity to help our kids. Let's make sure we do.

Of course, there are also many who transfer choice far too slowly. This is where *ability* greatly exceeds the *opportunity*. I have observed this recently in the context of a family-owned business. A strong-willed grandfather started the company sixty years ago. His fifty-five year-old son, supposedly acting as president, still has to check with Dad before buying a new coffee machine. In turn, the twenty-seven year-old granddaughter who manages the shipping department is treated like a teenage summer-hire. Very few multi-generation family businesses function smoothly. Why? Because one generation is unable or unwilling to transfer choices to the next. The old founder learned to do everything the hard way through trial and error. Having paid such a price for success, he is reluctant to hand the company over to his offspring who has not had to develop ability through the refining fires of hardship. Part of this, I suspect, is because handing over choice is a signal that his time is through. That must be hard to deal with, just as *any* situation in which there are diminishing choices is hard to deal with. Indeed, it may well be one of the most difficult challenges for any leader.

167

Do you remember when organizations used to talk about "empowerment?" What was intended, but seldom realized in that movement, was the redistribution of *choices*.

Learning to accept and make choices is one of the most complicated and difficult aspects of life. This is because the freedom to make reasoned choices is the defining factor in our humanness. And nothing is more difficult than becoming fully human. I believe that "maturity" can be defined as that point when an individual has finally accepted the full responsibility for the choices of his or her life. When one's abilities and opportunities not only match but are aligned in a miraculous and divine way, one's "contract with the Universe" is displayed in *living* color for all to see.

In addition to ability and opportunity, choice is linked to two other important concepts: responsibility and power. These are familiar concepts, but let's see if we can gain new insight into how they relate to the choices we make. If you are going to give choice to someone, you must also give them the responsibility and the accountability that goes with it. Not to do so is to aid in throwing that person's life totally off balance. So if you give your son the full choice to spend his weekly five-dollar allowance as he pleases and he blows it on an arcade game within an hour of getting it, does he get another five dollars to get through the rest of the week? The failure to attach responsibility and accountability to choice is like letting your kids drive a car without brakes.

I groaned when I read an article about some woman who is suing a credit card company because she believes it shouldn't have given her such a high credit limit. What absurd thought process is going on here? She foolishly and recklessly spent more than she could afford and so the credit card company is responsible and accountable and she's not? Call me up for jury duty on that one! I would serve with pleasure.

Should you be required to wear a helmet while riding a motorcycle or wear a seat belt in the car? What about strapping babies in the back seat where there are no air bags? Should you be restricted from smoking in a restaurant? These are the endlessly debated questions of day-to-day life and every one of them is a matter of choice, responsibility and accountability. More than that, we have to come full cycle and return to the notion of "co-participation."

If you choose not to wear a bike helmet because you love the wind whistling through your hair, I say, "Ride that iron!" But if you flip out and now feel the wind through your brain, don't use other people's tax dollars to pay for the reconstruction of your head. If you want to smoke, suck away! Just don't exhale. Because when you do, I have no choice about getting toxic substances into my lungs and, consequently, being hurt by you. Yet, as avid an anti-smoking freak as I am, there is a minute part of me that wonders about the fairness of smokers suing tobacco companies. When one picks up a product with a big label that reads "This will kill you" and uses it anyway, I have the urge to hand that person responsibility and accountability along with the lighter. One of the television preachers had a terrific line when he pointed out that if a can of dog food had a label reading "This product will give your dog cancer and maybe even cause death." you would not even *think* about feeding it to her. And yet millions of people breathe in their own destruction.

Not only do responsibility and accountability come along with choice, so does power. I believe choice and power are synonyms. The only people in our society's

Institutions who have any power are the ones who get to make choices. Everyone else is subservient and impotent. The more choices you get to make, the more power you have. The fewer choices you have, the more power-*less* and controlled you are by others. Again, this is why many people become so irritated by the Institutions of their lives – the power distribution system has taken away their choices and thus threatened their very humanity. After all these years of helping organizations, I have concluded that the issue of power – who has it and who doesn't – is at the heart of virtually all organizational problems, whether that organization is a family, church, school or office. How much power do you have in your life?

Am I advocating a world in which everyone gets to make whatever choice they want? Not by a long shot. If that were ever to become the case, I wouldn't want to live in such a world. Humankind has spent far too many years in anger, greed, selfishness and jealousy. We couldn't handle total freedom if we had it. That opportunity would exceed our collective ability. We need many of the structures and rules our Institutions impose on us.

Furthermore, basic group dynamics provide evidence that we are more likely to accept Institutional limitations if we are part of creating them. When *I* lock the door I feel secure and safe. When *you* lock the door on me I feel frightened and confined. When I set certain limitations I view them as being of essential value but if someone else were to set the very same limitations, I would feel that my "rights" were being violated. I would rise up against whatever power had dared to do this thing. This is exactly the battle gun control people are having with groups like the National Rifle Association. Some people want a three-day wait period before someone is able to purchase a gun.

The NRA wants a person to be able to buy a gun when he decides he wants one, or, at worst, with only a one-day wait. Is there something inherently evil in a three-day wait? Do law-abiding citizens buy a gun thinking, "I've got to shoot something *right now!*" Of course not. The gun control fight is over who is limiting whom. It is all about who has the power over choices.

Sometimes we call participation in defining limitations on choice "democracy." As a group we elect law-makers and expect that they will create the kind of Institutional control we want and are prepared to accept. Sometimes it actually works that way and sometimes it doesn't. Even when it doesn't reflect our wishes we think it's a better option than dictatorships where most people have no influence whatsoever. We like to claim that we live in a *free* world. The truth of this is something that we should be truly grateful for and yet I am not sure we have mastered the responsibility of freedom for all at all.

What I am advocating is a world in which our Institutions are wiser and more generous in granting choice to their membership. Everyone, in every Institutional context, needs to have a growing circle of opportunity in which he or she decides how creation can become real through the choices made.

When that circle expands beyond one's ability, creation is compromised. When that circle contracts to be smaller than one's ability, creation is also compromised. But when ability is aligned with opportunity in one's life, one starts to feel the power of being fully human and part of the creation story. Making choices gives you power and puts your life into motion. Making *wise* choices moves your life purposefully toward fulfilling your contract with the universe.

The key is to make choices. Every one of us has a backlog of choices we have been avoiding. Some of them are relatively minor and inconsequential. You've got to decide when you are going to take the car in for its 50,000 mile check. The odometer reads 72,600 miles. You have more files piled up on top of the file cabinet than you have in it. You need to make a choice about when you are going to straighten up your office. The world is not going to disintegrate if you put these choices off for another month. However, if your car breaks down half way to the airport and you miss your flight, or the file pile scatters on the floor giving you an even greater mess to sort out you are likely to get an, "I told you that would happen" from some helpful person.

When you *fail* to make the choices before you, the universe somehow "ups the ante" a little. Let's say everything you've read recently tells you that at your age you should go in for complete medical check-up. You choose to do so and the doctor detects the early signs of a potentially serious problem. You don't choose to do so and five years later you hear those awful words, "There's nothing we can do." It's too late for choices to be made.

Other choices involve our connections with our co-participators. At every turn we brush against other human beings trying to find their way and make their own choices. In these innumerable brushings, sometimes we have made the right choices and sometimes we have not. This is where the universe is gracious to us. When we do make the right choices, we usually have some experiential evidence confirming that we did so. We choose to be actively friendly to our elderly neighbor and discover in that relationship a source of wisdom and experience that saved us from making a very bad mistake. We chose to have a heart-to-heart discussion with our boss very early in our working relationship that became a foundation for a twenty-year partnership. We look back at how fragile some of these choices were and our heart floods with gratitude that somehow we made the right ones.

Four-time Pro-Bowl linebacker Chris Spielman made the right one. When his wife Stefanie found she had breast cancer he chose to sit out the season in order to help her fight the disease and care for their kids. She is now cancer-free and they have started the Stefanie Spielman Fund for Breast Cancer Research. Their lives are directed toward helping women make a choice about self-examination and mammograms. Says Chris, "We can't turn our backs because awareness and research could save my life, it could save my daughter's life, it could save my neighbor's life." Here is a family who acts on the responsibility of co-participation.

Of course the universe also provides evidence when we made the wrong choice. With visions of a quick fortune we unknowingly invest our savings with a scam artist. Or we show anger to the driver who pulls into the parking space we were just about to occupy, only to discover that she is the person interviewing us for a job we desperately want. Everyone has a story like this. We look back at the choices we made and we kick ourselves. What were we thinking?

One of the best stories of a person making a choice when the universe gave opportunity comes from my friend and fellow speaker, Sue Hershkowitz. Sue was flying home to Phoenix from a speaking engagement. She wasn't looking for opportunities to make choices but someone else was. Across the aisle from her sat Bill Coore, a golf course designer who had recently moved to the Phoenix area. As they exited the plane he said to her, "I don't mean to be rude, but you are one of the most beautiful women I have ever seen and I would very much like to meet with you if you are willing." Apparently this bold behavior is most unusual for Bill and why he chose to take the chance on this occasion is a mystery. But the end of the story is that seat 3B married seat 3D on December 28, 1997.

Of course, the most consequential choices of all are the choices you make in the journey to discover why your life exists. What is the purpose of You? Choice is the God-given tool with which you are to dig for the irreplaceable treasure, the answer to the most difficult question in the universe. Every seemingly inconsequential choice in your life sheds light or shadow on that divine purpose. That is even truer of the major choices of our lives. Because we seldom know at the time which are minor and which are major, *all* choices need to be treated as "opportunity gifts" from God. Treat none of them with disdain or ambivalence, because you just don't know the whole story.

Now here is the part that amazes, frightens, excites, challenges and energizes me. Can you imagine God (or the universe, if you prefer) giving us a divine meaning to fulfill and *not* also giving us some built-in sense, an innate wisdom, to recognize which choices will lead us to it and which will lead us away from it? Think of it as human software. We often buy software X, which happens to come loaded with programs Y and Z as well. They are "bundled" because we need the combination to get the most creativity and fulfillment out of the software. Likewise, *everything* we need to find and fulfill our life's meaning is already "bundled" into our lives for us. I believe that we already know, deep within us, which choices are the right ones for our particular destiny. I realize that often it does not seem like we do, and indeed that is part of the problem we have with choices.

Our minds and hearts fall somewhere between being like swamp water and pure glacial water bottled at the source. I have a bottle of the latter right beside me. The label says it comes from "protected locations with water of remarkable quality and purity." It even has a little picture of a snow-covered mountain with an arrow pointing to the actual spout the water came from. Unfortunately, as has been said, our choice-making is swamped by all too human foibles of greed, selfishness, hate, insecurity, lack of faith, narcissism and lust. Hold up a glass of swamp water and you will see all the impurities floating around in it, making it most unattractive. At first glance no one would even think of drinking it. Still, within that same glass is pure water, hidden among the contaminants. Put it through the right filters and you will see that this is true.

The same holds true for the choice-making of our lives. There is a purity of choice within each of us. We were created in the very image of God with all the rightness that implies. We were "bottled at the source." So where did all these contaminants come from? I think it began when human beings stopped loving God with all their heart and their neighbor as themselves. We tend only to love ourselves. It is very hard to balance a life on only one leg of a three-legged stool. The very wisest choices we can make are those that give homage to God and to a universe of brothers and sisters. In doing so we ultimately give homage to ourselves.

"Well thanks for the advice, your holiness!" you might be thinking. "Who died and made you Pope? It's a dog eat dog world out there. Other people are determined to get me, to beat me at my own game. What am I supposed to do, just pretend it's not happening?" This is the hard part. All we have is power over our own choices. That may not seem like a world-changing truth, but it is much more powerful than we think. Just one choice made to serve God and our neighbors purifies the water a little. Many choices made with this intention purify the water a lot. This is all we can do. And it is enough.

Depression can be a signal of pending choice as well. I am not talking about the complex and chronic depression that afflicts so many people, but the rather common "bad-hair-day" depression we all experience periodically. One way to look at depression is to see it as *anger turned inwards*. Why do we get angry at ourselves? Because we have a choice to make and we are not making it. Remember that irritation and anger always point to a choice that needs to be made. Let me take a greater risk and suggest that deep down inside we know what the right choice is in these situations. Oh, we protest that we don't because that would mean we actually have to *do* something. But we know. Everyone reading this has a decision to make right now but isn't making it. Yes, I'm in there too. Some of our choices are incidental and some are huge. I can't tell you the right timing for your choice, I have enough trouble knowing when to make my own. I just know that we regain control over our lives when we start making choices.

In my more righteous moments, and at the front-end of a choice, I try to reflect on *why* I want to do what I am about to do. *Why* do I want to make this particular choice? Does this choice bring benefit to God, to my co-participants, or just to me? I remember being criticized in front of a group by someone who did not have the correct information and misunderstood my role in that situation. At that moment I had to make a choice as to how to respond. The first reaction was to look after my own stature and reputation, preferably at the expense of his. That would have contaminated the water even more because then he would have to defend himself by attacking me again. I wish I had a dollar for every time I've made the wrong decision in similar situations. However, this was one of my righteous days and I made the choice to honor this man, and by extension the entire audience, by reacting with gentle explanation and not defensiveness or an attack.

In the days when I was just beginning to do international work, I was offered an exciting opportunity to conduct a series of seminars and speeches for a major international firm. I told my contact my fee, which was modestly set to ensure I would be hired. To my amazement he said, "Your fee should really be..." and he named a *higher* amount. I couldn't believe it. He could have hired me to his own economic benefit but he chose to honor me with his choice instead of taking advantage. I have been working with Philip Kirkby for many years and have tried to honor him and KPMG every time I open my mouth on their behalf. When we finally learn to bring honor to each other rather than seek advantages for ourselves, the world will begin to change very quickly.

Our personal relationships work or don't work depending on whether or not we choose to honor one another. The traditional marriage vow has a couple promising to "love, honor and obey." The first two reflect a spiritual connection, the third reflects the control-bent Institution. I have been in a relationship where there was little honoring and know that that is a miserable way to live. As you may have assumed from my several comments about my wife Georgia, we have a relationship with almost nothing but honoring of one another. It is just more fun and fulfilling to put the other person first.

In the closing lines of this chapter, I want to bring together three notions: *ability, opportunity* and the wonder of *knowing*. The "knowing" component you will recognize as the Seventh Secret. *You are on the right track with your life when the connection between your abilities and opportunities are endorsed by a divine sense of knowing.* You can remember the choice formula this way: When is a choice "**A-OK**?" When *Ability* matches *Opportunity* and is validated by a *Knowing*. It is not enough to have just ability and opportunity meet. I know this to be true. On a few occasions I have accepted a speaking engagement that I knew in my heart I shouldn't accept. There was nothing wrong with the client; the occasion was just not meant for me. Still the *opportunity* dropped into my lap and I had the *ability* to speak. Aren't two out of three enough? No, they are not. Probably I needed the money and that blurred the fact that I *knew* it wasn't the right engagement for me. We have all used the phrase, "I should have *known* better!" Well I did know better, I just didn't listen to that still quiet voice that was trying to get my attention.

I have a friend whose much-loved wife passed away a little while ago. Gradually gathering up his life again, he met a very wonderful woman. As nourishing as that has been for him, I think it also created its own tension. Was it too soon? Was he being disloyal to his late wife? What would he want if the situation had been reversed? You can imagine the kind of questions one would ask oneself in this situation. I asked him where he was in all of this. He told me, "I have a *knowing* about her." What a loving and wonderful way to put it.

The best and wisest choices are those in which the opportunity matches our ability *and* we have a knowing. This is what gives power to our life and testifies to all our co-participants that we are indeed essential to the crowning of creation and that the universe cannot be complete without us. And then, once again, God will look down on creation and say, "It is good."

Choice is the bridge to our divine calling, our contract with the universe. Choices are steps toward – or away – from a truly meaningful life.

What Is the Meaning and Purpose of My Life?

You can find the answer to the most difficult question in the Universe.

ACTION SEVEN

This is where the rubber hits the road, the point where you step toward or away from your destiny. You can philosophize, meditate and even pray about your future, but until you take the step and make the choice, your life will be slipping away. What *choices* are you prepared to make today?

In the concluding chapter you will find interviews with various people who have found their destinies. In every case, as they told their stories to me, they would stop at various points and say, "I had a choice to make..." They would then go on to describe the choice, what influenced it and so on. Your life and my life are no different. Life is lived choice by choice by choice.

Even if you have given only a cursory glance at the various "Actions" at the end of each chapter, I'm sure you noticed that you have been making choices all along. A quick review of them will more clearly illuminate the choice point you now face.

Action One had you choosing which of the "co-participators" in your life seemed to truly care about the fulfillment of your destiny and which were actually distracting you from it. You were also encouraged to keep your spiritual antenna sensitive to new co-participators entering your life. For some readers this first Action step would have been, and probably continues to be, very difficult.

Action Two was even more introspective. Here you were invited to look at your life against the template of the Six Spiritual Stations. The intent was for you to see clearly just what hand you have been dealt in terms of the various experiences of your life. This Action step may have begun to identify where you are restless in your life, a discovery that is essential to discovering your life's meaning.

Action Three took the restlessness and the irritation in your life and shined a spotlight on them. Again, you had an invitation to choose those dimensions where you know the world and your life are not right. Rather than tranquilize these irritations, I suggested you see them as the major guideposts to your destiny. These first three Actions provided a broad panorama of your life.

Action Four asked you to get a more detailed view of your life, and tried to bring you face to face with the specifics of your current reality. You were asked to chose five aspects of your reality that seem to weigh on you the most and to wring out of them every drop of learning and insight hidden inside.

Action Five called you to the wonders of a richly imagined future in which your life is filled to overflowing. Using the Seven Secrets as a guide you got to choose some imaginings about the most important yearnings of your life and to send those pictures out to the Universe.

Action Six asked you to make both incidental and major choices that would disrupt the routine, security and comfort of your life in dimensions where you are stuck and perhaps unable to answer destiny's call. When destiny asks you to dance, I hope you will be ready. Destiny does not take rejection very well.

Your Assignment

Action Seven simply asks you to step over the line and declare a significant choice or two that will move you to a life fully filled with divine and passionate purpose.

If this book has been even mildly successful in fulfilling its intention, at least one or two choices that have been fermenting deep within your soul will have surfaced. Amidst all the fears, rationalizations, joys, hurts, needs, longings and ambiguities of your life, your destiny calls to you. I hope our time together has turned up the volume!

When I was a teenager my friends would often greet each other with the question, "Whadda ya know?" Back in those days, when purpose was not even close to being discovered, when the most difficult question in the Universe was rarely asked, the answer was usually, "Nuthin'." Now that we are all at a different time and in a different place, maybe the updated version of the question bears repeating: *What is the meaning or purpose of your life and what are you choosing to do to fulfill it?*

Answering these final questions will help you bring all of this together. You matter to this universe. This is your time to step up to your own destiny. It is your time to declare to all those around you that you are ready. And most important of all, it is your time to feel the joyful power of spiritual freedom that comes with knowing you are meaningful.

What choices are you prepared to make in your life _right now_?

1. _____

2. _____

3. _____

As best as you can express it right now, what would you say your destiny is?

_____

_____

_____

Chapter Eight

LEARNING FROM THE WISDOM OF OTHERS

I mentioned Scott Peck's estimate that only five to ten percent of us have a sense of destiny. If you accept that, you are also likely to agree that we personally know very few people in this tiny minority. Do you know anyone who truly and confidently knows the "Why?" of his or her life?

You cannot identify such a person by how many academic degrees he lists after his name. For too many of us formal education has had precious little to do with our life's purpose. Nor can you identify the "destined" by notoriety or celebrity. Too many celebrities live sad and pointless lives for that to be the criteria. Riches? I don't think so. Being rich does not mean a person has found his destiny. We are more likely to view the wealthy as manipulative and self-seeking rulers of our Institutions. They may be *driven,* but that is not the same as knowing one's *destiny.* Lots of driven people have no destination. They just go until they run out of gas. But, at the same time we have *absolutely no right* to conclude that a driven, educated and wealthy celebrity cannot know the "Why?" of his or her life. Indeed I am not sure we can develop a "Destiny Test" enabling us to know who has found it and who has not.

My experience is that even the most focused of us bounce like a Ping-Pong ball between "I know my life's purpose" and "I don't know what I am doing." Even a world changer, as evidenced by Christ himself, goes through moments of feeling his destiny is just too great to bear. It is too fearful. It is too heavy. He wants out of it. Life would be so much easier if we were to flee to an island somewhere and spend the rest of our days carving faces out of coconut husks or braiding beads into tourist's hair.

I have been able to find a variety of people who have found their answers. Since these people have a life of meaning and know their answer to the most difficult question in the universe, I wanted to see if there might be any consistent lessons we can learn from them. Some of these folks I have known for a while. They are treasured and regular participants in my life. Others I have been directed to by circumstances or by people who know and admire them. A few you may have read about in newspapers or seen on television because of their celebrity. Some will be strangers to you, at least initially. Before I introduce them to you and they have the chance to tell you how they came to know the purpose of their lives, I feel the need to emphasize that no claims to holiness are being made by anyone here. Far from it. All of them want you to know they will continue to seek meaning as long as they live.

Let me provide introductions. The first man is responsible for breaking my friend's thumb in university. Meet hockey legend Paul Henderson, the man who scored what we Canadians call THE GOAL. Picture the last game of the first Canada-Russia hockey series. Each team had three wins. The seventh game, tied, was down to the last thirty-six seconds. With Canada's pride at stake, Paul scored THE GOAL. When that happened my friend jumped so high in excitement he broke his thumb on the ceiling.

That was in 1972. Was that goal Paul's destiny? Yes, but only partly – it was really only one step along his way.

I was introduced to Terry Ribb by a mutual friend. At first she was hesitant about being in this book. "Compared to the other people you are including," she said, "I haven't done much. I don't have any degrees and nobody has ever heard of me." Now that we've gotten to know each other, I would gladly trade one of my degrees just to listen to Terry talk about her views on life and work. She knows what she is doing in this world, about that there can be no doubt. She works for Deloitte Consulting, helping to re-invent businesses that believe in, and act on, the creativity of their workers.

Third up is W Mitchell. The W stands on its own with no period after it because there is no period signifying a full stop anywhere in Mitchell's life. He has been through some horrendous events that, without question, would have finished most of us. They almost finished him, until he discovered a powerful secret. Mitchell and I differ a little in how we view the circumstances that come into our lives, which is why I learn a little more every time I talk with him. This is one man we simply *must* pay attention to.

The next person you will meet is Kevin Francis. When I sent him this manuscript and arranged to interview him, he was President of Xerox Canada. It added a little spice to our interview when I discovered he was restless about what he was doing. As he put it, he "wasn't having fun any more." As it turned out, he made a huge career decision, proving to me that this man walks his talk. He is now the President and CEO of JetForm, a company that develops automated business solutions. He has an amazing presence of leadership about him.

Every once in a while I meet someone who seems to ooze wisdom. Richard Thieme is just such a man. I find what he has observed about life and destiny so absorbing, I am literally left speechless. He is a former Episcopal priest who now speaks and writes in the technology sector. He houses an incredible mind and an even more incredible heart.

Calling this woman "different" is the farthest thing from an insult as you can get. Dyani Davis is in tune with creation like few people I have ever met. A Native American, Dyani is a Licensed Massage Therapist, a convenient label to use in superficial discussion. Fundamentally, she is a remarkable healer of people, animals and plants. She feels so strongly that what she does is her divine destiny that most of the people she helps have to argue with her to take money. She is a truly spiritual woman.

The American cowboy: Is there any existence more romanticized than that? Admit it; somewhere in your old family photo album is a picture of a little you wearing a red felt cowboy hat with the drawstring under your chin and a little vest with fringes. Meet Al Dunning. This cowboy works, eats and sleeps on the back of a horse. Al breeds, raises, trains and shows Reining Quarter Horses. A World Champion in that field, he has written best-selling books about it. He is a household name to anyone with dirt on their boots.

Each one of these ordinary people sees the divine purpose of his or her life extending far beyond the confines of a job description. They *know* who they are and why they are here and *that* is what makes them extraordinary. Thankfully, they are generous in wanting to share what they have learned about themselves. Let's meet them.

Paul Henderson

What is your current occupation? I mentor men as they deal with the issues of their lives and try to help them see how God truly cares about them.

Which teacher had the most influence on your life? He was a high school principal named P. W. Hoag. I was a real smart-aleck jock in Grade Nine and he sat me down and told me that if I didn't smarten up and use my abilities I wasn't going to accomplish anything. Then he just left me there to think about it. That's when I decided that maybe I should get a little more serious about what I was doing.

Which person had the most influence on your life? That would be a mentor, John Bradford of Birmingham, Alabama. He was the first man I met who was tremendously successful in business and also had a strong faith in God. Keeping an upright character in the midst of success is a great challenge. Not many people seem able to do it.

What is your most treasured book? Without question it's the Bible. I am really a big fan of the Bible; there's not a book that's even a close second.

Do you have a dream that is yet to be fulfilled? I have always wanted to write a significant and serious book on what it *really* means to be a Christian. There has been a recurring phrase in my life:

"Start Small, Go Deep, Think Big, Finish Well." The one thing I really want to do is "finish well!" The book would be about what I have learned about faith and God's involvement in my life.

What do you think of this book? The issues you address are not talked about nearly enough, especially your points about building your life around purpose and passion. And your thoughts on irritation were particularly powerful because it described me exactly. I saw my life in your book so dramatically. I also loved your honesty.

Ian: Paul, to any self-respecting Canadian – and probably to any real jock – your name is synonymous with that historic hockey series. Nearly thirty years later, Canadians remember where they were when you scored that final winning goal. Do people still ask you about that event?

Paul: Yes, almost everyday. You'd think the thing would go away, but I just spoke to a high school student body where highlights were shown. The kids were excited and asked all kinds of questions. And now that goal has been voted the Canadian Sports Moment of the Century so I guess it will stay in our memories for some time yet – at least in Canadian memories.

But you know Ian, I came to a point where I felt I had to either walk away from that experience or embrace it. I decided to embrace it. My life does not revolve around that goal, but it does help me connect to people and it opens them up to what I might have to say.

Ian: Your achievement was so huge in Canadian sports, that one might think, "Well, there's your destiny fulfilled. That will go down in the history books and you might as well fade off into the sunset because there is nothing left for you to do." I want to hear about your whole journey. But first, what was it like in the immediate aftermath of that series? Did you hit a vacuum of any sort?

Paul: It was a total vacuum! Maybe more like hitting a brick wall! All I really wanted was to have the good life. That goal gave me that and all the celebrity anyone could ever want. I have even been called a Canadian icon! A sports hero! But this experience still did not answer the question about who I was or why was I here. Celebrity does not give you those answers. There was something huge missing that I couldn't even articulate. I felt restless and irritated just as you describe in the book – *exactly* like you describe in the book! I'd try to talk to my wife and to friends and they'd look at me like I'd lost my mind. They would say, "What is your problem?" because it looked like I had everything one could want.

What I finally realized was that I had bought a bill of goods. I felt angry about that but even knowing *that* didn't help a lot because I still didn't know where to go. I didn't have books like you've written to help me understand. And I've got to tell you: what is really frustrating is knowing that you are irritated but not knowing what you're irritated at or who to fight. After all, from the age of fourteen, Paul Henderson was a "self-made man." I used to be so proud of that but then I started to wonder how I could be so smart and feel so empty and angry at the same time.

Then I began to see God softly moving in the background and I'm convinced he orchestrated the whole thing. I was so wrapped up in myself that it was the only way he could get my attention.

Ian: You know better than many the importance of what I called our "co-participators." It seems like much of your life has happened in the context of a team. Did that team in '72 share a bond, a sort of spiritual destiny, or were they simply playing hockey?

Paul: Initially we were just a bunch of arrogant "Lone Rangers" who were going to put the Russians in their place. The coach had one game plan; unfortunately, each player had his own game plan as well. Then we got the stuffing kicked out of us, to say the least. We hit a point where we just had to come together as a team or face embarrassment for the rest of our lives. In your book *Going Deep*, you called this kind of confrontation with reality a "shuddering" and that's what we felt. It became a matter of Democracy against Communism, the West against the East. It was a matter of fighting for Freedom. At the end there was a kind of spiritual bonding. Every guy out there on the ice would have done *anything* for the others. There was total respect for one another and we supported each other to the *nth* degree.

It was a tremendous struggle to get to that point but we did it and won the last three games of the series. We just got stronger and stronger. At the end, Phil Esposito said we could have kept playing forever and they would *never* have won another game. As I look back on it now, I think he was right. You wrote that we do not find or fulfill our destiny alone. That team was sure proof of that.

Ian: Paul, what I have learned is that no matter how grand one's accomplishments are, there are a thousand little ordinary choices and experiences along the way that made it all possible. Would you outline some of the key turning points of your own journey?

Paul: One of those experiences comes to mind right away. When I was eighteen I had made up my mind to quit hockey. I wanted to finish my education because I was petrified about being poor. In fact, I had already notified the Detroit Red Wings that I was going to leave. But my dad sat me down and said that when I watched the game on television and the players skated out on the ice, I would always wonder whether or not I would have made it in the NHL. For the rest of my life I would wonder. Suddenly I realized that my fear was keeping me from realizing my dream. I talked it over with my girlfriend Eleanor. She felt the same way and said that I should try. So that five-minute challenge from my dad led to everything that happened to me, as far as professional hockey goes.

And I guess the other big thing for me was meeting and marrying Eleanor. You wrote about our connections being "God-sends;" she was that for me, literally. I told her on our second date that I was going to marry her. She was fifteen and I was sixteen. Eleanor is just so filled with common sense. I credit her for everything I've been able to accomplish. I thank God everyday for her.

One of the other major turning points came for me out of my wrestling with whether or not to pursue Christianity. Eleanor and I were in Switzerland with Ron and Jan Ellis – you remember him from the Toronto Maple Leafs – and we had made it to the top of a mountain and were looking down at the clouds and over the glaciers. I mean it was incredible. I said to the others, "There has got to be a God, and I'm going to find him." There just had to be a purpose to all of this and I spent the next two years searching and reading until I came to a point where I chose to make God the center of my life.

Ian: In those supermarket magazines you often find a "Where are they now?" feature. What is your life all about now and to what degree do you feel a real *meaning* in what you are doing? I guess I am particularly interested in how you relate your sense of destiny in '72 to your sense of destiny now.

Paul: I have known since 1981 that God has a specific intention for me. At first I thought I was destined to be a church pastor but after a few months in a seminary I knew that I would never make it. Then I found out what missionaries make in salary and I almost died. My dream was to cut a large and successful swath through the business community but I was afraid that somehow God would crush me if I wasn't obedient to him. It took until 1986 before I found where I fit. And now I feel that I have the perfect job and can hardly wait to get started every day.

The goal I scored in 1972 gave me a profile that allowed me to build relationships with men in the business community. So in a very real way, my past point of destiny is very much related to my current point of destiny. What I do is establish men's groups of about ten members each. They meet regularly and the men talk about living a balanced life, about being husbands and fathers, about faith. These groups grow to be so open and honest and, generally, they struggle with the issues that men struggle with. And we do that without judgment of one another and without the formal structure that can keep some of these people out of an organized church. We are all a work in progress and are coming to see the world in a new way.

Ian: We mentioned "celebrity" earlier. Sometimes people equate that with having a destiny. How do you think celebrity relates to having a purpose in life?

Paul: God doesn't need celebrities. What he wants is a humble spirit. I think there is a Hall of Fame in heaven and it is filled with moms who instilled respect, love, discipline and purpose in their kids. It is filled with millions of unsung heroes only a few have even heard of. I may have become a celebrity because of a single goal I happened to score, but I'll tell you that brings its own weight. I am watched all the time. All it takes is for someone to hear me use the wrong tone to a waiter in a restaurant and I become a negative image to that person. You can do one thousand things right and one thing wrong and it is the one wrong thing that will make the papers. It took me awhile to become aware of that. Being a celebrity might open a few doors for you, but what really counts is what you do when you walk through them.

Ian: One last question, Paul. A young person comes up to you with a dream of making a significant impact on the world like you did and are doing. What insight and wisdom can you offer?

Paul: First of all, it is absolutely essential that we be dreamers. In your words it's having a "richly imagined future." When I meet someone who isn't a dreamer, I encourage that person to take some time to sort themselves out and to find what might have gone wrong. That is like the pilot light going out on your furnace. The most important thing is to get that dream alive again.

Secondly, always be a seeker. I don't want people to be unhappy where they are in life, but I do believe we are meant to always be looking around to see what else is out there. In that sense don't be complacent or even content about where you are. There is more.

Then, as I have come to understand it, recognize that life is largely a spiritual experience. It is the spiritual dimension that puts everything in perspective. I am not arrogant or clever enough to try and convince people that God exists or that Christianity is right. I just know that it is right for me. It has helped me get rid of anger and bitterness. We are all wounded in one way or another, and we all need to find what will help those wounds heal.

Fourth, live with gusto! Risk for your dream. I was so fearful of poverty I almost gave up my dream of playing in the NHL which I had had all of my life. I started practicing my autograph when I was in Grade Five! Fear will keep many people from fulfilling their dreams. That is a battle all of us face at some point.

Finally, and I particularly make this point when talking to teenagers, find someone who loves you and who you love. This is the whole secret. You were so right when you wrote that we cannot fulfill our destiny alone. We need the love of God and we need the love of others, more than we need anything else.

Ian: And so your destiny is…

Paul: My destiny is to use the celebrity God gave me as a way of connecting to businessmen in order to help them discover just how much God loves them.

Terry Ribb

What is your current occupation? I'm a Senior Manager for Deloitte Consulting. I look for ways to re-invent businesses so they involve the creative, untapped power of their people.

Which teacher had the most influence on your life? I'm sorry to say that not much of my formal education made sense. It didn't seem to apply to real life. I had a high grade point average in high school but couldn't write a business letter. Once in the real world, I had to start all over and look after my own education.

Which person has had the most influence on your life? That's my mother, Gloria Lee, who believes in miracles and who believes that everything is possible. Also my husband Doug who truly understands how the world works. While I tend to live in my dreams, Doug connects me to the workings of the earth.

What is your most treasured book? I have learned mostly from the journeys and insights of Albert Einstein, Charles Darwin, Norman Vincent Peale and Ralph Waldo Emerson. But my most treasured book is *Every Man a King* by Orison Swett Marden. It was published in 1906 and I bought it in a used bookstore for $5.00. I don't know anything about

its origin. It describes how your thoughts allow you to do anything.

Do you have a dream that is yet to be fulfilled? I long to create a democracy of ideas on earth. Today we live in a society where the "experts" own all the ideas. But the truth is that as the world changes, each person's situation, time and place becomes new. Their own ideas are the true answers to their new situation, time and place. My dream is for people to believe in their own ideas and to share their discoveries with others.

What do you think of this book? At first I didn't think the discoveries described in the book were right, at least for me. But when I traced back over my own life experiences, I realized it was the truth. I have even asked a few friends to trace their own life experiences in the same way. When they do, they are able to recognize why they are here on earth.

Ian: Terry, at first you were a little reluctant to be part of this book project.

Terry: It wasn't that I was reluctant so much because I was really pleased to be asked. It was more falling into the old trap of comparing one's own accomplishments to other people's accomplishments. It is so easy to think that people of destiny, as you put it, must have done something almost supernatural - saved the world from disaster, invented a vaccine or something remarkable like that. They are always written about in history books or they are household names. In my heart I know that is not true, because I know there is divine purpose to my life.

Ian: Tell us a little about your life. Can you point to a handful of critical events or circumstances that shaped who are?

Terry: This sounds strange, but I had a sense of purpose very early in life. Even as a child I was purpose-full, so-to-speak. Before I tell you about the major turning points of my life, let me bring up a phrase that has become central to everything I've done. You wrote about the "Irritations" of our lives and how those seemingly angry and restless experiences can actually provide the direction we need. I think that was one of the most important things you said in the book, though I use a different word for it. Carol Bly talked about "moral indignation" in her book *The Passionate, Accurate Story: Making Your Heart's Truth into Literature.* I see my life as having been a series of these "moral indignations" starting when I was very young.

For example, in Sunday school, I'd see pictures of the disciples with Jesus, all of them just standing there with little children around them. I remember thinking "Why aren't they out helping others?" Or I remember seeing a movie about some women going into a convent and I again wondered why they weren't out helping people instead of sitting in a dark convent all day. I actually felt this moral indignation about why people weren't helping each other more.

Ian: Where do you think that came from?

Terry: I'm not sure. I remember feeling this indignation as clearly as I feel indignation now as an adult. It was very powerful for me as a child.

Ian: Does this mean there are other moral indignations that have also brought your destiny into focus?

Terry: Actually there are several. One horrendous experience happened when I was quite young. My family situation was awful. It was filled with fighting. When I was about five or six, my parents went through an absolutely terrible divorce. I remember thinking, "This is crazy. I want nothing to do with this." Again, I had this indignation about how they were treating each other. It just wasn't right. That all climaxed when one day I walked into our bathroom just as my mother was cutting her wrists, trying to committing suicide. Frankly, I just disconnected myself from the whole scene. I just wanted to distance myself from them and that whole situation. I should quickly add that my mother is fully and happily alive and is a wonderful influence on my life.

Ian: It is hard for any of us to imagine what that experience must have been like for someone so young. How did that experience impact on you later on?

Terry: I got married right out of high school, determined to demonstrate that human beings could trust and help each other. In other words, the exact opposite to what my parent's experience had shown me. At the same time I realized that it is not enough just to have moral indignation. There I was, with minimal education and absolutely no skills that I knew about. I didn't even have any goals. So what I began to think about, in the absence of my own goals, was what other people's goals might be, and to come to a real understanding of *their* goals. Not only that, I started to invent ideas that would help them be successful in achieving them.

Ian: Is this when your passion about helping other people really took shape?

Terry: Yes. I really knew I wanted to change the way the world works, because how it seemed to be working was awful. But I am not through with my moral indignations yet.

In the years after high school, I was either involved in, or was very close to, four situations in which I, and many others, were laid off of our jobs through no fault of our own. I became intensely indignant about how people were treated in those situations and particularly at how hundreds of people's lives were put at risk by corporations that wanted only more profit. What got me was that no one seemed to care at all because no one was doing anything for these people. Again I put all my energy into trying to invent ways in which corporations could keep and protect their people, rather than carry on so destructively.

Ian: How did you do that?

Terry: In one of my jobs, I helped create a consulting process designed to find the *real* cause of the problems the company was facing. Most of the time business people react to the most visible aspect of a problem and immediately leap to the quickest solution. Sometimes the "fix" actually becomes the seed of what becomes an even bigger problem than the one they started with. Corporations conclude that they are not making enough money and that they have to lay off people, almost in the same breath. They don't think it through and they pretend they have no choice in the matter. No one takes the time to understand what might really be going on and learn how to use the ingenuity of those same people to solve the problem. Consequently they end up under-resourced. The workers are dis-spirited, customer service disintegrates, quality is laughable and down and down they go.

I believe that what is missing in these companies that are laying off people all over the place is a lack of vision. In your language, they don't have a "richly imagined future." When you have a vision centered on making the world a truly better place, the products and services that will make you a financial success will be drawn to it.

Right now I am working with Deloitte Consulting in developing a practice that shows companies how to develop new markets so they can continue to protect and care for their employees. One of my roles is as a Chief Innovation Officer for the Western United States, where I help other front-line workers like myself gather and share our discoveries and ideas. We want to help build companies that actually put people first, not just have that as a marketing slogan. Those that do so will enjoy great prosperity. We *can* change the way in which the business world works!

Ian: I really believe you are right. I heard you were putting some of your ideas into a book, it that true?

Terry: I am doing some writing about these ideas. A while ago I helped create a book called *Corporate Kinetics* by Michael Fradette and Steve Michaud. That book focuses on what the business world needs to be doing in order to be more positively relevant to our world. The key is to have nothing in the way of workers being able to respond flexibly and fast to the changes around them. Right now I am writing my own book that applies these principles to individuals so it is a more personal book. I'm planning to title it *Everyone is a Genius: How Your Ideas can Change the World.* For me "genius" is not about what you *know*, it's about what you are *learning.* Anyone who is learning and creating ideas is a genius. The key question is, "What is your vision of the world?" Once that vision is in place, each person's destiny is to create the ideas that will make it a reality.

Ian: Can you summarize your perspective on this whole issue for us?

Terry: First, create kind of an inventory of the things you are morally indignant about. They provide a very good clue about what you should be doing with your life. What unfairness bothers you? Where are people being treated badly? Your list will point you to where the world is not right and just might be the signal to your spirit that you should start changing things.

Second, don't run ahead of your life. Look at the moment you are in and ask your self, "What is the best thing I can do *right now?*" The power of your life is held in your goal and action in the immediate moment. Don't run ahead to the "moments" that might be coming way down the road when you haven't dealt with the moment you have in front of you.

Third, recognize that these moments will grow as you learn to trust and learn to be responsible. More and more of the world will open itself up to you.

Finally, remember that everyone has a closet full of "stupid things" – poor decisions made, inappropriate actions taken, negative and hurtful attitudes, and so on. Sometimes I wish we could see each other's real journey because we would see that all our lives are filled with a thousand little moments, some of which we have accepted with faith and responsibility and some we have not. Some things in our closet we would rather not talk about, yet they too have made us who we are. As you wrote, we are all the same; we are all co-participators. We have each been given a piece of the canvas to paint. Rarely do we see major flashes of brilliant accomplishment. That is not what destiny is all about as far as I understand it. It is always the little things that add up to something wonderful. I guess they add up to be the source of a life of meaning. Destiny is about those moments when we decide right then and there to make the world a better place.

Ian: And so your destiny is...

Terry: My destiny is to change the way the world works. I will always be trying to figure out exactly what that means and what part of the world I will have the chance to influence. So it is not a concrete thing for me, it will always be developing.

W Mitchell

What is your current occupation: I'm an author, speaker, broadcaster and traveler.

Which teacher had the most influence on your life? I don't think I could pick one.

Which person had the most influence on your life? My stepfather Luke Mitchell. He showed me how to be a gentleman, with the emphasis on "gentle." I'm still learning that lesson and am sometimes frustrated by how long it takes.

What is your most treasured book? *In Wildness is the Preservation of the World* by Eliot Porter with the words of Henry David Thoreau. I read it and later it was read to me in the hospital when I couldn't see. I am still seeking to understand its meaning fully.

Do you have a dream that is yet to be fulfilled? I yearn to find the life partner who will help me help her.

What do you think of this book? This book has made me think a lot about how easy it is not to see the other point of view.

It has caused me to question. It's given me a push.

Ian: It is pretty obvious that you have been through some horrendous experiences. You've been burned and you've been paralyzed. What happened?

Mitchell: I often talk to audiences about how my physical situation once formed a prison for me. My story is really about how I learned to break free from this prison. And you are right. My circumstances are pretty obvious because they are external. But over the years I've learned that it's the *internal* prisons of a defeated spirit, negative attitude, lack of courage and poor self-esteem that are the most difficult to break out of. Lots of people are caught behind those bars. Let me give you the nickel version of my story.

I was a relatively macho, man-about-town kind of guy. For most of my life I had been known to do the unusual and try almost anything. That got me into a lot of trouble in my early years but it was that adventurous kind of spirit that would prove to be my salvation later in life. To further enhance the macho image, I purchased a Honda 750 motorcycle, which, in 1971, was about as "hot" a bike as one could get. I was the self-proclaimed King of San Francisco riding around on that bike. But, one time, as I drove along South Van Ness, a laundry truck swerved suddenly, cutting me off. I crashed violently into it, crushing an elbow and my pelvis. The real damage came when the gas cap fell off, spilling gasoline all over that hot engine. I was caught in a fireball that was visible for blocks. Someone from a car lot nearby ran over with a fire extinguisher but I was severely burned over 65% of my body. Twenty minutes later the bike was still too hot for the tow truck people to handle. I have no memory of that experience and I hope I never do. Frankly I was a horrific mess.

Ian: I have read your remarkable book so I know you are skipping most of the details. You had to have your face reconstructed, you lost your fingers and generally had to endure indescribable pain and endless surgeries. Did you not just want to die to escape it all?

Mitchell: Talk about an understatement! Actually, I thought I had died. It is fortunate that in those days after the accident, I did not know how truly terrible the situation was. You wrote about "co-participators" but in my case "angels" is a better word. They are the ones who showed me that there was still a life to live. If it hadn't been for the love of a few people who cared unconditionally for me, we would not be talking in this nice hotel today.

Ian: Your recovery and rehabilitation were not the only big bumps on the road for you, were they?

Mitchell: I refused to be the prisoner of my physical limitations or my appearance. I still had the adventuresome spirit that I had had as a youngster. Six months after being burned, I was taking flying lessons again, working toward getting the pilot's license I had always dreamed about. And eventually I got it, which, when you don't have any fingers, is no easy trick. In 1975, four of us were flying in my plane from Gunnison Airport in Colorado to San Francisco. I had just gotten the plane airborne when it stalled, falling flat back down on the runway. Because I saw that the fuel tanks had spilled, I yelled for the others to get out, which they did. But when I tried to move, I couldn't. My legs wouldn't respond. It wasn't long before I knew that my twelfth thoracic vertebrae had been crushed and I would be spending the rest of my life in a wheelchair.

Ian: You have an incredible story and yet in a strange way I get the feeling that the "story" is not what's important.

Mitchell: The story isn't important, at least not any more than anybody else's story is important. What happens to us is what happens to us. The central theme and message of my life is that, "it's not what happens to you, it's what you do about it." Gratefully, I learned how to break out of my prison. We all have to break out of our prisons. Somewhere in your book you warned us about becoming trapped in our anger rather than using it to do something wonderful with our lives. We all get "breached" over and over again. Before my accidents I could do 10,000 things. Now I can only do 9,000. I can focus on the 1,000 things I can't do or focus on the 9,000 I can. It is pretty obvious which approach will lead to happiness and success, isn't it? Even though I focus pretty positively on my life and my work, frankly I'm not sure if I have a definable destiny or not. What I want to do is create a meaningful and pleasurable life for myself and in some small way help other people do that for themselves, too. As I think about it, even what I mean by "meaningful" changes all the time. When I give a speech, I want to say something that will touch someone. But I also want to accomplish something meaningful financially. And at the same time I want meaningful relationships, too.

Ian: In the context of your experiences, my point about our "co-participators" influencing our life seems a little trite. It sounds silly to say that, "I suffered severe burns because a co-participator drove a laundry truck in front of my motorcycle." But when you think of all the circumstances around your accidents, do you ever get angry at the people who were part of creating those events?

Mitchell: I was a participator in what happened to me and so were a number of other people. But what is the point of spending your life in blame? What has happened has happened. This is hard point to get to for a lot of people, but in reality, and unless you are a lawyer, it doesn't matter who is to blame. That just becomes another prison.

But now that you have brought it up, this is a good a time to talk about anger. You used quite a lot of your book in dealing with this issue. Though I am not proud of it, I showed my anger in many ways and, in fact, that temper has caused considerable difficulty in my most intimate relationships. What hurts the most, as I think about it, is how angry I would get at the very people who most loved me and who had sacrificed so much to care for me through these two accidents. Gratefully, over the years I have finally gained the insight that only *I* am responsible for how I react to the circumstances that come into my life. Anger is one of our choices all right – but there are much better options.

So let me make sure the whole point is being made here. In no way am I saying that we are not *responsible* and *accountable* for our choices and actions. The only person who can decide where my next step is going to land is me. Sure it hurts when bad things happen to you. Sure there may be some things you can't do anymore. But the next step is still yours. No one can take that away.

Ian: Do you believe there is a reason why things happen to us?

Mitchell: You wrote a lot about that and I understand the point you were making. I think I differ from you on this one. These things don't happen for a *reason*. I am not going to spend time trying to find the *reason* I happen to be in a wheelchair. I don't think there is a *reason* somebody gets sick. Things are happening to all of us all the time. Finding a reason isn't going to change that reality. Instead I think, "Now that I am in a wheelchair, what am I going to do?"

I feel the same way when wonderful and pleasurable things happen. We'd all go crazy running around looking for a *reason* for every event in our lives. What do you do if you can't find one? Hibernate? All of life gets down to the choices we make. To me, that is the really important point. It *is* our choices in life that create our richly imagined future.

Ian: Tell us about some of those "angels" you mentioned earlier, the people who turned out to be the key influencers in your life.

Mitchell: A very important few come to my mind right away. The first is my stepfather Luke Mitchell. He died when I was seventeen, but he taught me lessons about decency and fairness that have never left me. If we all treated people with decency and fairness, the world would be a dramatically different place.

The second person who turned out to be a huge influence on me was a neighbor of mine when I was twelve. His name was Dewey La Rosa. He was confined to a wheelchair. He was incredibly self-sufficient and he showed me that life can work just fine even from a wheelchair. I didn't know at the time how important he would be as a role model.

A third person is a saint of a woman I often call my "adopted mother." She is really my ex-mother-in-law and she cared for me during my long recovery. Her name is Beatriz Bernal. I don't know anyone more giving and selfless. Honestly, I wouldn't be here talking to you if it weren't for her and the love she poured into caring for me.

I want to mention someone else, whose name I can't even remember. Back when I was still in my "prison," I heard her talk about being responsible for what happens to you and I remember deeply resenting her message. I actually found myself angrily railing against this message. Of course, it was exactly the message I needed to hear. She said it was easier to look out the front windshield at where you are going because it is so much bigger than looking in the rearview mirror.

Ian: I know there are many others, all of whom have contributed to whom W Mitchell is today. You live a very full life. You were the mayor of Crested Butte. You ran for Congress. You've met presidents and movie stars. You are a phenomenal success as a professional speaker, traveling all over the world. And you have done all this against the greatest odds. People must come up to you all the time asking for your counsel about how they can make the most out of their life. What do you say?

Mitchell: I talk about the bumps in my life and how difficult they were. I talk about how dearly I wanted to quit and how richly I deserved to. But I also point out some other truths and if indeed I have a "destiny," perhaps sharing these is what it is all about.

- Pain is inevitable, suffering is optional.
- Do what you can, with what you have, where you are.
- Ask for what you want. People may say yes.
- Adversity introduces us to ourselves.
- We find only the world we look for.

Ian: And so your destiny is...

Mitchell: To demonstrate to the world that it's not what happens to me, it's what I do about it.

Kevin Francis

What is your current occupation? I'm the President and CEO of JetForm, Inc.

Which teacher had the most influence on your life? Bernadette Francis (no relation), Grade Nine, in Riverdale Rural High, Coxheath, Nova Scotia

Which person had the most influence on your life? My dad, Joe Francis. He taught me to dream big and to believe in myself. He also taught me the importance of family and used to take me to his business meetings across Eastern Canada.

What is your most treasured book? Believe it or not, I didn't like reading books, because I'd get bored. Magazines and newspapers were more to my liking because they are short and to the point. The books I do read tend to be nonfiction.

Do you have a dream that is yet to be fulfilled? Some part of my life will be devoted to public service.

What do you think of this book? The interrelations between business realities and spirituality are striking. Passion in business is no different than passion in life. This book transcends both worlds well. It's a good read.

Ian: Kevin, after about two minutes of conversation with you, it becomes pretty obvious that you give out a kind of contagious joy about your work. So many senior corporate leaders today seem so stressed

out they've become depressing to talk to. Where does your joy come from?

Kevin: One of the most often asked questions of me is: "Why are you always smiling and so energized?" My answer is always the same: "It's better than the alternative!" I get a special thrill from watching others grow and then succeed in achieving their ambitions. So to me, leadership is one of the most rewarding roles you could ever be given. Hiring, training, motivating, developing and promoting people on your team is what it's all about – it's the height of "co-participation." To provide leadership is to define extraordinary possibilities that ignite passions in others. For me this provides the greatest satisfaction. I guess I just believe that you need to be joyful in everything you dedicate yourself to or why would you bother to get involved?

Ian: Would you say finding joy and satisfaction depends on the specific company you work in, or is it more about the general opportunity to provide a meaningful kind of leadership to hundreds of people that most energizes and excites you?

Kevin: It is not company-specific because I felt that satisfaction for years at Xerox and now I feel even more energy and excitement here at JetForm. The secret has more to do with understanding the human spirit than with *where* you work. Universally, all people yearn to do things that provide meaning. As you've said, the idea of "meaning" is simple and complex at the same time. It is complex because we will never get to the point where we truly understand what makes people tick, why they do what they do, or even what it is they truly want out of life. At the same time, the human spirit is so tender and simple that a few words like "thank you," "well done," "excellent," or "great effort" have an incredible power to unleash creativity and the movement towards one's destiny. Of course a few words can also suppress the human spirit as well. All we want, when you get down to basics, is the love and loyalty of friends and family, and meaningful work. Describing it is simple, getting it is complex.

Ian: Kevin, you are a respected leader in the upper echelons of the corporate world. You are financially secure. You have a great family. You are a happy guy. You seem to be in a situation that most of us aspire to. Some might say, "You have it made!" What would you say to that?

Kevin: I am not sure anyone "has it made." That sounds like you are done, that there is nothing else to do. My path has not been all that easy and it does not take much to remind me about some of those rough times. I remember the excitement of deciding to join Xerox years ago. Sharon and I were engaged at the time and we were both thrilled with this opportunity. I was absolutely committed to get ahead in the company, starting with wanting to be the youngest branch manager in the company's history. Sharon and I said we would go anywhere, take any promotional move and do whatever it took to realize that goal. We moved back and forth across central and eastern Canada and finally I was appointed branch manager for one of the branches in Vancouver, British Columbia. I was twenty-nine. Sharon and I had two sons under the age of four and we had moved six times in six years.

I was a young and inexperienced manager trying to learn how to manage my time, helping others do their work effectively and, of course, trying to get my own work done. Fourteen-hour days weren't doing it so I began to work on the weekends as well. Then, in 1980 as part of a cost-cutting initiative, Xerox closed one of the Vancouver offices and I lost my job. The company offered me a position back in

Toronto. When I broke the news to Sharon, she broke down crying. Nothing is more important to Sharon than friends and family and she puts down roots deeper than anybody I know. Her reaction made me confront a very hard reality. I had worked my way out of our little family. I was no longer part of it because I was never home.

Ian: The discovery of the damage really wakes you up, doesn't it?

Kevin: I was shocked to see what had happened to us, all in the name of trying to be a success. Sharon said she couldn't face another move and I had to come to terms with the imbalance in my life. For a guy who lives his life by setting goals, I had lost my real purpose. I chose to resign and make my family my only priority. Fortunately the president at the time didn't want to lose me and decided to keep my branch open for another year. That gave us some breathing room and we did move back to Toronto, having agreed between us that we would not move again until the boys were of university age.

Ian: You did rise to the top of Xerox Canada and you are now at the helm of JetForm. Do you regard this business success as the major accomplishment of your life or, to be more dramatic, as the fulfillment of your destiny?

Kevin: A short story might help here. When I applied to work as a sales trainee at Xerox, I was asked to put on the application what I wanted to do. I wrote, "Be President." The interviewer wasn't quite sure what to do with this brash twenty-three year-old. I explained that I was brought up to believe the if you really wanted something, you needed to have a clearly defined goal that stretched you. I figured that, even if I didn't make it, having that goal would give me a context that would make my work purposeful. Twenty-six years later I became Chairman, President and CEO of Xerox Canada.

I am proud that I worked to fulfill that goal, no question about it. But I am prouder of the success of my family. Sharon and I have watched our two sons grow, graduate and begin their own business careers. I couldn't be happier about anything.

Ian: Why do I get the feeling we aren't finished with your story yet?

Kevin: You asked if I had fulfilled my destiny. That is a really pointed question for me because I recently became aware that I was, once more, in a soul-searching time of my life. I found myself searching for a new goal. Destiny is not a matter of obtaining a title or position; I learned that back in 1980. I felt like I had this list and all the things on it were checked off. Frankly that felt a little intimidating because I have always had something to reach for. So while I may have accomplished some pretty high goals, I didn't have a feeling of having fulfilled my destiny. I believed there was something in my future I had yet to discover.

Ian: So obviously you faced a major choice in your life. How did you go about that?

Kevin: I am convinced that it starts and ends with the simple question: "Am I having fun?" Admitting that I wasn't having fun any more was very difficult to do because I had put so much of my life into the success of one company. I know the idea of making a major career choice based on having fun sounds almost frivolous, but let me tell you another story. After my son Kirk graduated with a degree in engineering, he went on to a degree in architecture, something he had been interested in since he was very young. It was a cooperative program, so after his first term he went to work in an architectural firm. One day he came home looking glum, saying that he hated his job and that he didn't know what to do. We talked about what he *loved* to do. He was most excited when talking about problem-solving, planning change, and having a variety of dynamic things to work on. For him, consulting seemed to be a better fit. He left architecture to become an analyst with a major consulting firm. He has found both meaning and FUN! This story is not about one profession over another – it's about finding a purpose and a role that is fun. I want that for my family, for every one of my employees and, of course, for myself. I can't help others have fun unless I am having fun right along with them. I have found that "fun" again at JetForm and it's given me a wonderful surge of energy, excitement and expectation.

Ian: But we both know that having fun it is not always easy.

Kevin: Of course it's not easy. We wouldn't want it to be. The trick question is: "How do you tell the difference between the normal ups and downs of life, and the true realization that the *fun* is gone out of what you are doing?" I am not sure I have totally figured that out yet but having started a new chapter of my destiny, I think I'm a lot closer. I believe that somehow your soul guides you quite well in this regard if you take the time to listen to it. The "knowing" will come, I am sure.

Ian: And so your destiny is...

Kevin: To provide corporate leadership that results in people have fun doing meaningful work.

Richard Thieme

What is your current occupation: I'm a speaker, writer, and thinker.

Which teacher had the most influence on your life? There are several, but if I had to pick one I'd say Richard Ellmann, who was a James Joyce scholar at Northwestern University. He was not only brilliant and wise but treated me, and everyone else, with real compassion and respect.

Which person had the most influence on your life? I'd have to say my mother, who raised my brother and me as a "single mom" long before it was fashionable. My father died suddenly when my brother and I were very young.

What is your most treasured book? *Ulysses* by James Joyce. I think Joyce was the number one writer of the last century.

Do you have a dream that is yet to be fulfilled? I would like to combine all I have written in one book, to bring together the passions of my mind and to make a difference.

What do you think of this book? I think your book stands out as genuine wisdom and spiritual insight. You have reflected deeply, thoughtfully and helpfully on the critical issues of our lives. There is a lot of stuff out there that pretends. You are real and I regard you as a fellow traveler.

Ian: Richard, before we get to the twists and turns on your road to finding meaning, let me ask an obvious question. You spent sixteen years as an Episcopal priest and then decided to work and write in the field of technology. When you hear of someone "leaving the priesthood," you often assume that somehow God let that person down. What was at the heart of that major transition for you?

Richard: This is a complex question. What I can tell you is that I am equally sure that God called me *out of* the pulpit as I am that God called me *into* it. I absolutely believe that *any* platform is a "pulpit" and that the "grace" of our work is not contingent on the hierarchical structure or authority of an organization. It is about being truly grounded in who you are and coming from that point with integrity and courage. The thread that binds all the parts of my life is a passion for truth and justice. The "truth" came from literature and the "justice" came from my commitment to God.

When I left the Episcopal ministry a parishioner said, "I just have to know; do you still believe in God?" My response was, "There is no question in my heart that God exists, but that does not mean things are not as bad as they look." There is injustice everywhere and the challenge for all of us is to do the right thing. When we don't, we surrender to the injustice and "they" win. The only weapon we have is truth. Everywhere I have gone, whether the church or the corporate world or elsewhere, I see a capacity for evil. But we cannot have a passion for fighting and exposing injustice unless we have another benchmark. For me, that benchmark is that evil is not the ultimate bottom line. Evil will not triumph. Does that make sense to you?

Ian: Yes it does. So your personal destiny revolves around establishing truth and justice. The various roles you have played, and will play, are simply how you have dressed to fight that battle. What I want people to see is that *first* you choose the battle, the cause or purpose that will bring you fulfillment, and *then* you choose the uniform, career, position, location and so on. I think too many people try to do it the other way around and never do find the cause for which to fight. When did you first have a real sense of destiny or purpose to your life and what led to that discovery?

Richard: When I was ten or so. Part of my "destiny awareness" may have been compensation on my part. My father died when I was two years old, so part of my sense of destiny and deep connection to God may also have been protection against the absence of a father. What I feel is that my involvement in the church and becoming a "Father" was a bulwark against loss and death. It is not lost on me that I left the priesthood at the age of forty-nine – the same age my father was when he died.

The truth about "meaning" in relationship to spiritual reality is that either it is totally and fully possible, or it is not possible at all. Likewise, either God is found throughout the entire universe or he is not to be found at all. Having said this, the fact that I felt a sense of purpose either meant I had indeed found the fullness of my divine destiny – or I had not found it at all and was simply manifesting a compensatory mechanism to protect myself against emptiness and meaninglessness. Both are possible explanations.

Even as a child I experienced a "light," an experience of the mystical connectedness and oneness of all things. This went away during my adolescence, but in my twenties I had a profound transformational experience that taught me from the inside out what "conversion" experience is all about. Conversion requires us to let go of one thing in order to take hold of another. It's the psyche coming to the end of its way of holding itself and letting go in order to restructure at a higher level of organization. This is what Jesus meant when he talked about being "born again." You have to go through a zone of annihilation in which you confront the inadequacy of everything you think yourself to be in order to re-discover your Self at a deeper level. Unfortunately, some people go through a break with the Self but do not find anything else to attach to. That's why they feel a void or vacuum in their lives. I found something else to attach to. I knew I would never see the world the same way again, and I never have.

The "connectedness of all things" is not a metaphor. It is literally true. Those who know this can live out of that knowledge with a higher intentionality. If we are open to the invisible world and to what everyone is putting out always anyway, then our responsibility is to be putting out love. That was your first "Secret" as I recall. People are getting what we are putting out whether we think they are or not, or whether we notice it or not. Therefore our responsibility is to be as loving as contributors as we possibly can in our lives. That is what will make the difference.

Ian: Do you believe *all* of us are created with a divine purpose or destiny? Let me add on an even more difficult question before you answer. The other day I watched television coverage of the famine in Ethiopia. Starving people were picking single kernels of wheat out of the dirt. When I see that, to be really honest, what I am writing about seems rather pointless. Do those poor people in Ethiopia have a divine destiny, too?

Richard: I agree with you that we *all* have a divine destiny. But what do we say about your second question? We watch news of a plane crash where ninety-nine people die and one survives. The survivor rightly feels that God was with him or her. But does that mean the God was *not* with those that died? Does this mean that somehow those who died did *not* have a destiny while the survivor did? Of course not.

Despite the pain, the horrors, the injustices and the seeming meaninglessness, we have to stand on our square foot of earth in our one moment of shining light and declare, "This is meaningful!" The greatest onslaught to that stand is the voice of the devil who says, "You are kidding yourself, it's not meaningful, there is no point." We live on the edge between the one voice saying, "It is meaningful." and the other voice saying, "No it is not." The struggle is made more intense because there is much more evidence of meaninglessness than there is meaning, just like there is more evidence for the crucifixion than there is for the resurrection. Is it any wonder, then, that knowing your destiny is a most difficult task? We think for a moment that we know, and then we don't.

Ian: Do you foresee yet another change in your life's meaning in the future? And how do you know – I mean really *know* – that a redirection is, in fact, the wisest thing for your life?

Richard: The question really is, "How do you know that you know?" and you explored that in the book. I have learned that if you are going to open a new door, be sure it is the door you want to go through. And another thing – be careful about doors that won't shut. The key is to let the evidence of "rightness" come in and to have enough skepticism so that you don't run ahead of that evidence. For me there is growing evidence that my writing will become increasingly more important as I fulfill my destiny. In the midst of my confidence about this direction, however, I am also aware that 98% of what seems to be evidence for my choices is illusionary. This is true for everyone. You gave the example of how we justify buying a new car and how we work very hard to find evidence that we should do so, and that is exactly the point I am reaffirming. What we need to do is find the 2% of real evidence, the gold nugget hidden in the ore. I try to use all of my faculties to discern what is right, but really it is all intuitive, when you get down to it.

Ian: You have a remarkable background in literature. Can you think of a reference that, as far as you are concerned, "says it all" about this matter of meaning and destiny?

Richard: I immediately think of the words of the prophet Micah: "O man, what *is* good; and what does the Lord require of you but to do justice and to love mercy, and to walk humbly with your God?"

Ian: Richard, you have people all over the world seeking your counsel and wisdom. What would you say to someone who feels aimless as far as the purpose of his life goes?

Richard: I don't tell anybody anything. What I do is try to get them to open up and explore. One tool that I have used for twenty years is known as "An Exercise in Personal Intentionality." This is not my creation but it is extremely useful, because, in truth, I have no advice to give.

What I suggest is that people write each of the following titles on the top of a page, returning to add to it as often as necessary until complete. This exercise illuminates the direction and momentum of the arrow of your life and enables you to set the arrow more securely in the bow of your intentionality.

Communications I need to deliver:

Things started and not being worked on:

Things I want to have and don't have:

Things I want to do and am not doing:

Things I want to be and am not being:

Things I want to complete and am not completing:

Things I have wanted to experience and haven't experienced:

Things I have wanted to have and don't have:

Things I want to stop and am continuing:

Things I wanted to be and am not:

Things I wanted to do and have not done:

Things I have wanted to accumulate and haven't:

Things I wanted to start and I haven't started:

Things that I wanted to change that I am not changing:

Things that recur and won't stop:

Things I can't get started:

Things about which I am dissatisfied:

Things that are incomplete for me:

Things I wanted to say that I don't know how to say:

Things I wanted to say that I don't want to say:

Something that I am holding on to:

Something I am resisting:

Something I am afraid to look at:

Ian: And so your destiny is…

Richard: To find truth and then to write and speak about it so that justice will prevail. I believe that once we are committed to finding the meaning of our life, all sorts of remarkable things happen.

Dyani Davis

What is your current occupation? I can tell you about the things I do, like work with animals, give people therapeutic massages, help people with strokes regain movement, give out information about health and balance – but I don't classify myself by a job. Every morning when I get up I ask the Spirit to lead me to a person, animal or plant that needs my help.

Which teacher had the most influence on you? I really can't name one because I see teachers all around me. I am taught by my elders and will be for the rest of my life. I am also taught by animals and plants and by canyons and mountains all around me. Everything in the universe can teach you if you are open to it.

Which person had the most influence on you? Again I am grateful for my elders, my fathers and mothers, grandfathers and grandmothers. In my culture we refer to all our elders as part of our family and that's why I refer to multiple grandparents and so on. We also feel the influence of our elders even though they have died, to the extent that we refer to them as though they were still alive. For example, my grandfather Sitting Bull is someone whose presence I feel frequently.

What is your most treasured book? *Everything is Sacred* by Little Crow. He taught me to respect all things because everything shares the same energy and everything is part of the same universe. When we hurt one part of it, we hurt ourselves.

Do you have a dream that is yet to be fulfilled? I want to do more to bring joy and hope to the world, to see more happiness.

What do you think of this book? I thought it was really powerful particularly because you talk about the connection between all things.

Ian: Dyani, tell us about your cultural background.

Dyani: I am Native American and have come out of a mixture of Chiricuhua Apache, Sioux, and then was adopted into the Yabapai culture. My mother died when I was born and I was raised by another family for a couple of years. When I was still little I was taken from that family and went to live with the wealthy woman Patricia Leonard. This happened to many of the children on the Reservation because we were so poor that this was the only way of getting any education. She treated me like she did her own children, sent me to the same school and really taught me to respect and believe in myself.

Ever since I was a child, I saw things differently. Because of how my ancestors saw the world, I too felt a connection with all things around me to the point where some probably thought of me as a little strange. Actually there were times when I wondered if I *was* strange. But I learned that often when people see things they do not understand, they criticize those who do see and understand. Little Crow confirmed that I was not strange just because I could sense things in people and animals. He was a great help to me. I know I am okay. This is the part of your book that was the strongest for me. We have to see that we do not go through life alone. We are part of everything, we are all connected.

Ian: In a deep and wonderful way, it seems that who you are and what you are doing is an extension of something much bigger than you, almost like you have a cultural or ancestral responsibility toward our world. What does your destiny look like?

Dyani: Like I said earlier, I get up everyday looking for an opportunity to help a person, animal or plant. I want to see happy people, animals, plants – a happy world. I want to see people find their specific purpose but the truth is we all have one purpose and that is to love everyone and everything. When we do, we feel the mysterious universal connection. This will be one of those strange sounding things, but I can connect to a withdrawn child or to an old man suffering from stroke. I can go to a barn and know if the horses are happy or not. I have been through a lot of hard experiences myself and even these things have helped me love and connect.

Ian: I know that you are always taking courses in various subjects and that you are learning all the time. But have you ever had the impulse to get a regular nine-to-five job, to do something different than you are doing now?

Dyani: I do not want to do anything that will minimize opportunities to help living things. Many jobs have nothing to do with loving and connection and happiness. Most jobs seem to make people withdraw, not reach out. The freedom I have to go where I am needed is something for which there is no substitute.

Ian: What gives you the most confirmation that you are doing what you are meant to be doing?

Dyani: Seeing a child come out of herself and begin to interact effectively with her world. Seeing a man who could not move his arm able to lift it over his head. To see an animal have new energy and joy. All such things are signs that the world is being restored to what it is meant to be.

Ian: You get intimately involved in people's health and well-being. Do you ever talk with them about the purpose of their lives?

Dyani: Yes I do, but only when I really feel I *have* to say something. I don't seek or ask for that particular involvement but sometimes I feel a direction from deep within me that I should say something. There have been times when I felt that impulse so strongly that I couldn't keep quiet or mind my own business if I wanted to.

Ian: Can I ask you what you would say to all of us about finding our divine destiny?

Dyani: In my culture we learned long ago that such answers come from inside. But in our modern world there is so much noise that most can't hear anything. We need to be in quiet places. The answers are inside. Listen.

Ian: And so your destiny is…

Dyani: To bring help to anyone or anything that needs it.

Al Dunning

What is your current occupation? I train horses. Actually it's a lot more than that. I write. I teach. Frankly, I do just about anything you can do around horses.

Which teacher had the most influence on your life? The teacher who comes quickest to mind does not come from my school experience. He was one of my first riding instructors, Jim Paul. I was twelve years old and didn't have a father around the house. He filled the gap. Jim was a real cowboy – chewed tobacco, got into fist fights, and the whole thing. But he taught me how to grow up and made me want to become a good and honest man.

Which person had the most influence on your life? There were two. The first, John Hoyt, was the guy who made me know I wanted to be a professional horseman. He taught me how to think things through and taught me the value of loyalty. Then there was Don Dodge, probably the greatest horseman of all time. He really influenced me with the idea that my business had to be more than riding horses

or I'd end up with little more than a box full of ribbons and buckles. I learned how to be a businessman from him.

What is your most treasured book? I've got to say it's the Bible. No "buts" about it – it does have the answers. I should read it more.

Do you have a dream that is yet to be fulfilled? I dream all the time so it's hard to pick something. I am addicted to riding horses and in every event I dream about winning. I guess if I had to pick something, I'd like to win the "World's Greatest Horseman" title.

What did you think of this book? I found it very thought provoking. It gave me a spiritual feeling because it's about how we relate to each other, to the world and to God.

Ian: Have you always been on the back of a horse?

Al: My sisters started riding when we lived in Chicago, but frankly, I was scared about riding. Then, when we moved to Arizona, we bought our first horse for $300 and I started riding all the time when I was about twelve.

Ian: To most people Al, your life seems romantic. While there is no question that it is real and hard work, to what extent do you really find meaning or an expression of "destiny" in what you are doing?

Al: The spiritual side of me needs to answer this. The Lord put me in this position so I could touch people's lives and in that sense this is my destiny. I teach riding clinics all over the world and meet many thousands of people. I want them to know that my happiness does not come from the horses but from my relationship to God. The meaning of my life lies in my ministry to people, and horses are just the vehicle for doing that. While I believe God wants me to do well, the meaning of what I do is not about income or visibility.

Ian: What circumstances led you to where you are today?

Al: We were raised by a single mom. Horses weren't part of our family history. When my sisters quit riding, I inherited their horses. I also met the right people like Jim Paul who gave me the guidance I needed when I needed it. And I will be grateful forever to have met the right woman. I knew I'd marry Becky from the moment I met her. All of these things gave me opportunities to make some choices and I was lucky enough to make the right ones. That is, at least most of time. Just after our first child was born and Becky was unable to travel with me so much, I made some not so good choices and ended up in a major horse accident. I remember lying there on the ground paralyzed from the waist down. You know the saying, "if it doesn't kill you, it'll make you a better person?" I saw this as a big slap on the head from God and I promised him that if he would let me get up, I'd become the kind of man he wanted me to be.

What I've learned is that the trials we run into and the difficulties we face can actually become some of the best "friends" we'll ever have and can make us better people. It's like you wrote about irritation and pain – they can point you in the right direction if you pay attention and listen.

Ian: You talked about key choices in your life. Was there a point in all of this where you almost went down a totally different road? And if so, what influenced your decision at that point?

Al: When I was studying in school I wanted to be one of two things, either a personnel director or a policeman. I was sitting in a music appreciation class at Arizona State University and I thought about my life. The realization that I would not be happy being indoors and that I was happiest with horses was so clear that I just left my books on my desk and walked out. That very day I asked Becky to marry me. At the same time I became a professional horseman. I wouldn't advise anybody else to do it that way but it worked for me.

Ian: That was a pretty courageous thing to do. You must have had people telling you that you were out of your mind and that you'd never make a decent living.

Al: I sure did – Becky's father for one! But I had thought about it and decided to go where I was happiest. Becky was right there all the way.

Ian: After all your success, do you ever have moments where you wonder if you are meant to change directions?

Al: I am totally clear that I am meant to be on this road. It is not what I do, it's who I am. But I am a thinker and have a lot of ideas. If I couldn't get on a horse I would easily do something else – but it would probably still be horse-related.

Ian: Throughout our conversation you have given the impression that this is much more than a business and income source, that it a spiritual thing.

Al: That's true even around the barn. I've been lucky enough to be able to surround myself with people who know what this is really all about, who know the true meaning of the horses. That applies to the man who cleans the barn as well as to me. Becky and I, along with those around us, are able to help a lot of people in many ways.

Ian: What in your incredible life has brought you the greatest joy and affirmation?

Al: My greatest joy is my family. I've got a wonderful wife and super kids. When I think of affirmation, I think of the old saying that "it's lonely at the top." I have come to realize that it's lonely at the top only if you are focused on yourself and not on others. Every victory needs to make us more humble and more excited at the same time. Every time I win a competition, I wonder, "Why me?" and just feel so grateful that, for whatever reason, I was chosen.

Ian: Al, suppose a young person came to you at a point where he was wondering about the most meaningful way to spend his life. What wisdom have you found that would be helpful to that person?

Al: First, go slow! Don't grow up too fast. Take your time and let God tell you what to do. Second, find something that makes you happy! Don't go after anyone else's dream, go after your own. Too often the "American Dream" is all about accumulation and power but there is so much more than that. Third, count your blessings everyday. Remember what is important and always be grateful that you are lucky enough to be able to do what you want to do. The fourth thing is to learn who your friends really are. You called them "co-participators" I think. It's true. Don't count your friends when you are on top of the world, count them when the world is on top of you. It is so important to get the right people around you.

Ian: And so your destiny is…

Al: To use horses as a way to reach and influence people. I want to touch people's lives.

This is your time!

Because we are so interwoven, we are meant, I am convinced, to learn from one another's journey. I sincerely hope you felt a connection with at least one of these stories about the search for meaning. Like all our stories, each is so familiar and yet so different. Destiny and meaning comes in many shapes, colors and languages. Did you notice how often it was the incidental experiences that had a dramatic impact on their destinies? While a lightning bolt of recognition does occasionally happen, it is usually a mistake to wait for it to strike. Rarely are we directed in such a dramatic, obvious way. If that is your expectation you will wait a long time while the world passes you by.

Meaning is present in the "small things" of life. It is the quiet voice inside that speaks to you. You have had a thousand little "directions" this week already. The challenge of life is to learn how to recognize and heed them.

We began our quest for a life of meaning by looking at those who surround us – our co-participators. They are so critical to our fulfillment, which is why we need to ensure that we participate with those who sincerely want us to find the meaning of our lives and who are able to help us do so.

Assuming this support, we explored the map of our inner journey, seeing that there is much more of a universal pattern than we may have thought. My hope is that, once we know the twists and turns of the inner spiritual journey more clearly, we will advance with greater boldness.

Along the way all of us will encounter irritation and anger because the road is difficult, with people and institutions threatening to tear meaning from our lives and experiences. For me, and perhaps for you, one of the biggest emotional and spiritual transitions is to see this anger as a divine source of energy that nudges us toward critical insights and choices.

At the heart of those insights lie Seven wondrous Secrets that, if we heed them, serve as signposts – pointing us to our life's meaning. What confidence and affirmation this should bring us! With the Seven Secrets safely in our souls, we face a very real world – a world that calls on us to change it by first changing ourselves.

All of that being said, not a single person can be forced to seek and find the divine meaning of his or her life. That is the choice of choices only you can make. And you would not be here with me if you had not already made it. You *know* you are destined for greatness. It is *your* time to make your presence felt in this world, whether you do so through planting gardens, filling the receptive minds of children, discovering a vaccine, fixing the brakes on a bus, or leading a nation.

It is time for you to stand tall and make the courageous choices your soul began to put before you even prior to your first breath. It is time for you to take your place among those who have answered the call of the Creator to come and complete creation. Go boldly. **It is your *destiny.***

OTHER HIGHLY RECOMMENDED EXPLORATIONS

James Autry – anything by him but especially *Life and Work: a manager's search for meaning*. New York: Avon Books 1994.

Richard Barrett. *Spiritual Unfoldment – A Guide to Liberating Your Soul*. Alexandria, VA: Unfoldment Publications. 1995.

Geoffrey Bellman. *Your Signature Path: Gaining new perspectives on life and work*. San Francisco: Berrett-Koehler. 1996.

Deborah Bloch & Lee Richmond. *Soul Work: Finding the work you love, Loving the work you have*. Palo Alto, CA: Davies-Black Publishing. 1998.

Frederic and Mary Ann Brussat. *Spiritual Literacy: Reading the Sacred in Everyday Life*. New York: Scribner. 1996.

John Dalla Costa – anything by him but especially *Working Wisdom*. Toronto: Stoddart Publishing. 1995.

Max De Pree – anything by him but especially *Leading Without Power*. San Francisco: Jossey-Bass. 1997.

Wayne Dyer. *Your Sacred Self*. New York: Harper Collins. 1995

Matthew Fox – anything by him but especially *The Reinvention of Work*. New York: HarperCollins. 1994.

Kay Gilley – anything by her but especially *The Alchemy of Fear at Work*. Newton, MA: Butterworth-Heinmann. 1997

Janet Hagberg – anything by her but especially *Real Power: Stages of personal power in organizations*. Salem, WI: Sheffield Publishing. 1994.

Sam Keen – anything by him but especially *Hymns to an Unknown God*. New York: Bantam Books. 1994.

W Mitchell. *It's Not What Happens to You, It's What You Do About It*. Arvada, CO: Phoenix Press. 1999.

Scott Peck. *Further Along the Road Less Traveled: the unending journey toward spiritual growth*. New York: Simon & Schuster. 1993.

Lance Secretan – anything by him but especially *Inspirational Leadership*. Toronto: Macmillan Canada. 1999.

Gary Zukav – anything by him but especially *The Seat of the Soul*. New York: Simon & Schuster. 1990.

ABOUT THE AUTHOR

I an Percy is one of North America's most thought provoking and inspirational speakers and authors. For over thirty years he has helped organizations around the world find new meaning in their work and influence. Few blend insight and unending humor like he does – and even fewer are able to touch audiences so deeply.

Born in Nigeria to missionary parents, Ian moved to Canada at the age of eleven. School was a constant struggle most of his early life with "C" being the height of academic achievement. Not until college did he begin to discover that just maybe, he too had a purpose. He was granted a degree in education and theology in 1969 and went on to undergraduate and graduate success in organizational psychology, becoming a Registered Psychologist in 1978.

A natural entrepreneur, Ian started his first company while still an undergraduate, providing training programs mostly to the health care field. Over the years his business and his speaking and consulting skills grew exponentially. Today he is in much demand by companies like, Microsoft, Transamerica, Xerox, Royal Bank, Union Central Insurance, Nortel, KPMG and many others around the world.

Ian has been honored as "One of the Top 21 Speakers for the 21st Century" by *Successful Meetings* magazine, and has been inducted into the Canadian Speaking Hall of Fame. He is a Certified Speaking Professional, the highest earned distinction granted by the National Speakers Association. In addition, Ian is a regular "performance improvement" columnist for *Human Capital* magazine.

Ian and his wife Georgia now live in Arizona, USA. When he can, Ian competes with his Quarter Horse, "Hollywood."

INSPIRATIONAL PRODUCTS FROM IAN PERCY

Going Deep: Exploring Spirituality in Life and Leadership (247 pages) Available in hard and soft cover. If you have ever driven into work on a Monday morning saying to yourself, "Why am I doing this?" then this book is for you. One of the most powerful and intimate business books on leadership you will ever read. Insightful and filled with humor. Renowned author Dr. Wayne Dyer describes it as "Sensational!"

Going Deep is also available as an **Audio Album.** 8 Cassettes, over 7 hours of inspiration and insight. Read by the author.

The 11 Commandments for an Enthusiastic Team is a 30 minute video of one of the most renowned motivational speeches of modern times. If this doesn't motivate your team to new levels of performance and unity, nothing will. Ask about the frameable posters that support the "*11 Commandments*" message. Also available as an audio cassette.

Yackity Yack ~ the game that's got everyone talking ™ If you have children 5 – 18 this incredible family board game is for you. Imagine a game that creates meaningful communication between children and parents and yet is so much fun it is the kids who will beg you to play it! Players "win" real treats or real chores! Described as, "the best thing to happen to the family since the kitchen table!" Endorsed by Kathy Lynn of *Parenting Today*.

All of these products and more are available at
Ian Percy's *Inspiration Store*.

To purchase these products or to enquire
about Ian Percy's services, go to:

www.IanPercy.com